James Samuel Stone

Simple sermons on simple subjects

James Samuel Stone

Simple sermons on simple subjects

ISBN/EAN: 9783337085889

Printed in Europe, USA, Canada, Australia, Japan

Cover: Foto ©Lupo / pixelio.de

More available books at **www.hansebooks.com**

SIMPLE SERMONS

ON

SIMPLE SUBJECTS,

BY THE

REV. JAMES S. STONE,
RECTOR OF ST. PHILIP'S CHURCH, TORONTO.

"𝔓𝔯𝔢𝔞𝔠𝔥 𝔱𝔥𝔢 𝔚𝔬𝔯𝔡."

TORONTO:
WILLING AND WILLIAMSON.
MDCCCLXXIX.

These Sermons

ARE AFFECTIONATELY DEDICATED TO

My Loving Friends,

THE MEMBERS OF THE TWO CHURCHES IN WHICH
I HAVE MINISTERED,

St. John's, Port Hope,

AND

St. Philip's, Toronto.

PREFACE.

THE nature of the book is such as to need very little preface. I may briefly state that the sermons contained herein are but simple utterances on simple, old-fashioned subjects. They were delivered during the past winter in St. Philip's Church, Toronto, and are now placed in this more permanent form at the request of many of the members and friends of that congregation. I commit them to the press with much diffidence. I am well aware that a style which is at all effective in the pulpit will rarely retain its power when transferred to the pages of a book. And when I remember that volumes of sermons are seldom read, even in these days of reading, I can hardly hope that mine will meet with any better success. But should there be among my readers one who may find in this book some truth, or some presentation of the truth, that shall in any way tend to his or her spiritual advancement, I shall be amply repaid for all I have done. I send the book out with the simple desire that it may be useful somewhere. I cast it as bread upon the waters; it may be lost out of sight, it may take root in some spot where I least expect it—I leave all that to God; I have done my best, the rest I have nought to do with, and whether it be His good pleasure that I should find it after many days or not, I am content. Only that it may by its quiet and unobtrusive ministry help forward the coming of the perfect Kingdom of God, by the gathering in of some soul to Christ, or by the strengthening of some weak believer, is all I ask. May the Master use it as it may seem best unto Him!

TORONTO, April 19th, 1879.

CONTENTS.

	PAGE
I. THE ETERNITY OF THE WORD	9
II. THE UNVEILING OF SECRETS	24
III. UNBELIEF	36
IV. THE MARVELLOUS CHANGE	51
V. APPEARING WITH CHRIST	65
VI. THE LOVE OF GOD	78
VII. THE LOVE OF THE LORD JESUS	92
VIII. SALVATION THE EFFECT OF MERCY	105
IX. THE VESSELS OF MERCY	119
X. THE LIFE OF CHRIST	132
XI. THE POWER OF CHRIST'S NAME	146
XII. THE GOOD GIFTS OF GOD	161
XIII. THE BLESSINGS OF FAITH	177
XIV. THE GUIDANCE OF GOD	190
XV. THE LAST REST	204
XVI. ASSURANCE	220

NOTE.—For the argument on page 14 I am indebted to a little work entitled "Bible Bulwarks," by the Rev. R. Newton, D.D., of Philadelphia; and for some expressions on page 100 to that wonderful book, "All About Jesus," by Alexander Dickson.

J. S. S.

Simple Sermons on Simple Subjects.

SERMON I.

THE ETERNITY OF THE WORD.

Isaiah xl. 8.—"The grass withereth, the flower fadeth; but the word of our God shall stand for ever."

THERE is something very sad in the rapidity with which Nature works her changes. The eye no sooner rests upon some fairy scene of rich luxuriance than like a dream it is gone. We behold to-day the landscape decked in brightest beauty—our gardens robed in flowery glory—tomorrow all has passed away—" the grass withereth, the flower fadeth." Wherever we go—to the rich farm lands, or to the violet-purpled moss-beds of the sequestered glen, or to the deep quiet retreats of the wild greenwood

"Change and decay in all around we see."

Winter's hand, like the cold hand of death, effaces all those glorious beauties. They were born but to wither and to die.

Amid all this change and desolation, however, the prophet declares that one thing remains unchangeable—" the word of our God shall stand for ever." That can neither wither nor fade nor die. It is eternal—refreshing and sweet to the soul, as is the green grass and the vernal flower to the eye, yet not like them short-lived, weak and changing, but forever and forever the same. This is what we should expect. Let us see how well it is supported —on what a firm foundation it rests.

That " the word of our God shall stand for ever" we are sure from what we know of the NATURE OF GOD.

The conception we form in our own mind of God is that of a Being who is the very absolute ideal of Perfection. This perfection is not limited, not finite, but boundless and infinite. We could not define it for the simple reason that we cannot grasp it. It is beyond us. The eye peers into the clear waters of the mid-ocean, but no sight can pierce those dark unfathomable depths; nor can the soul, though it rests its vision upon God ever so intently, penetrate the abyss of His absolute and infinite perfection.

This idea of perfection placed far beyond the ken of man is confirmed by the declarations of Scripture. "Your Father which is in heaven," says Christ, "is perfect." He is perfect in His *unchangeableness:* " with Him there is no variableness, neither shadow of turning;" He is perfect in His *omnipresence:* "do not I fill heaven and earth? saith the Lord;" He is perfect in His *omnipotence:* "with God all things are possible" And so with His moral attributes. He is perfect in His *wisdom:* "in Him are hid all the treasures of wisdom and knowledge;" in His *truth:* "His truth endureth to all generations," "He abideth faithful;" in His *love:* "God is love;" and in His *justice:* "He will render to every man according to his deeds."

God being thus absolute perfection we cannot conceive that He will not be perfect in all He says. "The word which I have spoken shall be done, saith the Lord God." "Heaven and earth shall pass away, but my words shall not pass away." If that which God has said should fail He would not be perfect. There would be either a lack of wisdom or power. Yet we know that the future is to Him as the present and that his power knows no bounds. Were it not so He would not be God—He would be finite, and limited in His operations.

Let me illustrate this point. God has declared that the punishment of the wicked shall be terrible in its misery and eternal in its duration. If there is anything in the Scriptures plain and certain this is. Yet men deny it and try to reason it away. They appeal to God's great love and mercy. He cannot, they say, allow His children, whom He loves so much, to go on to endless suffering. But He has said that the "wicked shall go away into everlasting punishment:" shall He contradict Himself? Shall He say that at one time which He may deny at another? Shall He declare that at one moment which some say is cruel and unreasonable and at another ignore His justice and forget His former statements? This would be to deny His perfection and to make Him appear as changeable, whereas we know that "the Strength of Israel will not lie nor repent: for He is not a man that He should repent." If He did it in this instance what assurance have we that He may not do it in others? Our very security rests upon His perfect unchangeableness: "I am the Lord, I change not; therefore ye sons of Jacob are not consumed." So that whether His word be one of threatening or one of promise "it shall stand for ever." If He said that which He did not intend to carry out, He would be deceiving us and His holiness would not be perfect; or if He said that which He could not carry out, a limit would be placed to His power; or if He said that of which He had not perfect knowledge His wisdom would be at fault. We cannot conceive this of God, for our conception of Him is of one absolutely perfect. It would be contrary to all that is told us of Him in the Bible. It would be the death-blow to all our hopes for we could not depend upon Him. We could not trust Him. Our future would be a dead, dead blank. Our joy would wither as the grass, our peace fade as the flower. We cannot imagine this of God. We cannot imagine Him as changing in His purpose. We cannot imagine Him as anything but the one unchanging, unchangeable and perfect Being. He cannot deny or contradict Himself. From what we know of His nature we are sure that though "the grass withereth and the flower fadeth, yet the word of our God shall stand for ever."

But, in the *second* place, we have a further confirmation of this grand truth in the HISTORICAL FULFILMENT OF HIS WORD.

There are some remarkable fulfilments of prophecy that convince us that the word of our God shall stand for ever. I will mention two of them.

The City of Babylon was one of the oldest in the world. It was also a city of superb magnificence, immense wealth, and vast size, and was, moreover, at one time the capital of a great and powerful empire. In the time of Isaiah, it was flourishing unrivalled in its beauty and strength, it was "the glory of kingdoms," and more than a hundred years afterwards, in Jeremiah's day, it was still in its unparalleled splendour; yet the Lord declared by the mouth of those two prophets that it should be overthrown as were Sodom and Gomorrah, and that it should become a desolation among the nations. Two thousand and six hundred years have come and gone since then, and that "great city," "the beauty of the Chaldee's excellency," has emphatically "become heaps" of ruins. Her walls have altogether disappeared—they have "fallen," been "thrown down," been "utterly broken." She is "a desolation," her "land a wilderness:" "wild beasts of the desert lie there:" and "owls dwell there;" and the natives regard the whole site as haunted, and neither will the "Arab pitch tent, nor the shepherd fold sheep there." Thus is the word of the Lord literally fulfilled.

You may say that this was but following out the course of time: that any. one could foretell that Babylon would come to an end. Perhaps so, but take an opposite case.

Jerusalem is a city of even greater renown than Babylon. If any city may be called Eternal, none more so. David declared that God would establish it forever; and marvellously indeed has it been preserved. In the fifteen hundred years preceding the time of Christ, it was besieged no fewer than seventeen times; twice it was razed to the ground; and on two other occasions its walls were levelled. Since then its people have been scattered, and it has passed from Roman to Turk, and neither Jew nor Christian have ruled in the Holy City for twelve hundred years. But Jerusalem stands to-day as God said it should, and thus His word is fulfilled. Surely there is something more than mere chance in this. Here we have two cities, concerning which, three thousand years ago, God declared that one should be destroyed and the other should be preserved, and we find it so to the very letter. Who but God could look over the history of thirty centuries yet to come? And if His word was thus accomplished in these cases, may we not reasonably suppose it will be in other instances?

But there is a most wonderful instance that furnishes us with an argument of great force. It relates to the marvellous preservation and universal dispersion of the Jewish people. In the book of Amos there is this striking prophecy: " I will sift the house of Israel among all nations, saith the Lord, like as corn is sifted in a sieve, yet shall not the least grain fall upon the earth." For eighteen hundred years the Jews have been scattered everywhere; despised, oppressed and persecuted in all lands, and yet preserved through all the ages, a distinct and peculiar people. There is nothing like this in the history of the world. No other nation has been driven from its fatherland and yet preserved its identity. No other nation has shown such remarkable vitality. "Empires, the most illustrious, have fallen and buried the men that constructed them, but the Jew has lived among the ruins, a living monument of indestructibility. Persecution has unsheathed the sword and kindled the faggot; Papal superstition and Moslem barbarism have smitten them with unsparing ferocity; penal rescripts and deep prejudice have visited on them the most unrighteous chastisement;" and yet notwithstanding all, they live. There is not a land where they are not. " The snows of Lapland have chilled and the suns of Africa have scorched them." " They are broken into fragments, scattered and peeled over the earth." And all this God declared should be twenty-five hundred years ago! If we want a fulfilment of God's word surely we have it here. No so-called scientific criticism can reason away facts as plain as these. As well say that there is no such thing as history, no such thing as life, that neither you, dear reader, nor I exist, as to deny that God's word concerning the Jews has not been actually and literally fulfilled. " The grass withereth, the flower fadeth, but the word of our God shall stand for ever." The preservation of God's ancient people, according to prophecy, is a proof we cannot dispute. It is a living witness to the eternity of the Word. And taken in connection with the multitude of other historical fulfilments, we need no stronger confirmation of the truth of our text. But this is an argument often used, and I therefore pass on.

In the *third* place I will appeal to our INDIVIDUAL EXPERIENCE AND OBSERVATION as a proof of our text.

I feel that our personal knowledge furnishes us with an argument equal in strength to any I have brought forward. Perhaps every one may not think so. .It is true one person's experience is of small account. A man may say, "To those who believe God has promised peace. I do believe and I have peace. I know that my sins are forgiven, and that I am saved through the blood of the Lord Jesus Christ. I fear no evil, my soul is full of joy." A sceptic might say, "the man may be mistaken, his convictions be mere fancy, and his mind disordered," and in such a case the man's evidence would be simply worthless. But suppose the peace and joy and hope which I find in this man I find also in tens of thousands, nay hundreds of thousands of others of all grades of Society—rich and poor, the most learned and the most ignorant—in every nation under heaven have I not an accumulated mass of evidence of immense value ? You may say that a drop of water is a small thing, not capable even of putting out a gas-light, but the accumulation of those little drops makes mighty oceans, and forms a force second to none in strength—a force that can rend great continents asunder, and bear upon its bosom vast navies, and set in motion the factory-wheels, the trains and the steamboats of wealthy empires—a force that can spread desolation over the land and sweep its thousands into the pit of death. You may ignore the single drop, but you cannot ignore the vast accumulation of untold millions. So you may doubt the evidence of one man, but you cannot doubt the evidence given by thousands and millions. We claim that Christianity can produce certain results among men, and we see those results produced everywhere and under all circumstances. A man is convinced of sin and led to the Saviour, and there finds life and salvation. He is a new man ever afterwards. His face beams with joy, his heart thrills with gladness, his soul burns with zeal. And what we see in him we may see any day in ten thousand others. In all ages, from the time God first revealed Himself to man this is true. And I say when we have before us a fact such as this— a fact which tells us that the experience of any one of God's people is also the experience of millions, and that the life which burns in one converted soul burns in ten thousand times ten thousand of other souls, we have an argument before us of immense strength—an argument that grows stronger and stronger the more we examine it. So that our individual experience and observation do come in to convince us that the " word of our God shall stand for ever."

Now, take any one of the promises of God : take, for instance, this one, " Come unto me all ye that labour and are heavy laden, and I will give you rest." There is rest promised to the weary and the sorrowing and the sinning—simply upon going to Christ. Have we in our own experience known that word to fail when we have gone in prayer to God ? Have we ever heard of any one who has failed to obtain peace at the foot of the Cross? Sinners have gone there bowed down with the burden of iniquity and found rest; mourners have looked from the grave of death to the Lord of life and found rest in Him; weak and trembling ones have found rest from their doubts and fears by looking from self to God. Let me give an instance of how God has fulfilled His promise of rest to the weary.

In the April of 1877, a flood of water burst into a coal pit in South Wales. It came from an old pit long disused that was close by, and rushed along the galleries with great force. Many of the colliers were saved, but when the muster-roll was called fourteen were missing. They had been working in distant parts of the mine when the flood surrounded them and cut off their escape. A number of men volunteered to attempt their rescue, and finally nine were saved, some of them after ten days of imprisonment in that dark, flooded coal-gallery. But an incident is related of five who were separated from their companions. When shut up in total darkness, expecting soon to die by starvation or drowning, the water slowly but surely rising around them, the memory of dear ones to be left behind filling their hearts with deepest sorrow, they took, as they thought, a last farewell of each other, and in their living sepulchre sang together in the Welsh tongue a hymn of which this is a translation:

> " 'Mid the deep and mighty waters
> There is none can hold my head,
> Save my dearly-loved Redeemer—
> He who suffered in my stead:
> He's a friend in Jordan river,
> He my head will hold on high;
> And by looking to my Saviour
> I can sing, e'en when I die."

They were God-fearing men, and was not God with them in their hour of need? "Come unto me," saith He, "and I will give you rest,"—had they not gone to Him and had He not given them rest—nay more, joy, and peace and hope? Surely the word of our God shall stand for ever!

In the royal palace of England, the great and good Prince Albert is stretched upon his dying bed. His wife, the loving and sorrowing Queen, sits by overwhelmed with grief. To see her there was not one of the least of his sorrows. Death cast its cold pall upon his love, his glory, and his life, but God was with him. Falteringly, he said, " I have had wealth, and rank and power, and I thank God for them; but if these were all, I should *now* be poor indeed." And then, as his spirit was passing peacefully away to its everlasting rest, he whispered these sweet words:

> " Rock of Ages, cleft for me,
> Let me hide myself in Thee."

There again we have God fulfilling his word. Instances of a like nature are unnumbered for multitude. To the simple colliers in the coal-pit, to the educated, refined and powerful prince—to the weary and heavy laden—to all alike, without respect of person, according to His word, He gives the fulness of rest, the fulness of the peace which passeth all understanding. We who are serving the Lord know all this to be true. We know in our own experience that not one jot or tittle of His word has fallen to the ground. We know that hereafter we shall hear "as it were the voice of a great multitude, and as the voice of many waters, and as the voice of mighty thunderings," the whole ransomed Church of God assent to the same grand truth. We do not question this. Our personal knowledge places it beyond our doubt. We may be very sure from our individual experience and observation, that, though "the grass withereth and the flower fadeth, yet the word of our God shall stand for ever." Can we, with this argument before us, and the argument derived from the historical fulfilment of God's word, and the one we have from our knowledge of His nature, come to any other conclusion than that the proposition contained in the text is abundantly and marvellously proved and confirmed?

If this be granted, an application of the truth is soon made. I need not dwell upon it. Surely it behoves us seriously and solemnly to lay to heart that God's word will be literally and truly performed. To those who die in their sins, who know nothing of a personal, living Saviour, there comes a day of terrible wrath; "the wicked shall be turned into hell, and all the nations that forget God." Listen, my dear reader, to those solemn words—the words of a God which shall stand for ever. We dare not ignore that awful declaration. We dare not dream that it will not be fulfilled.

But to those who are one with Christ—who believe in Him and are serving Him—what sure comfort and blessed assurance there is in this glorious truth! All that He has said will come to pass. His presence will be with us, guiding and guarding us; His spirit will be in us, perfecting and sanctifying us; His love will be around us pardoning our offences and drawing us closer and closer to Himself. All through life

> "His purposes will ripen fast,
> Unfolding every hour;
> The bud may have a bitter taste,
> But sweet will be the flower."

And at last, when the gloom shall fall upon our pathway and the eventide shall overtake us, the dark clouds shall be gilded with the glory of the setting sun—every tinted ray of golden light shall be to us a promise fulfilled, every rippling wave breaking at our feet the assurance that God is ever the same—and surrounded by the signs of His presence, we shall sink, overwhelmed by the waters of mercy, into the ocean of His love, to rise again on the other shore, in the land where there shall be no more night, no more sorrow, no more death—where we shall be forever and forever with the Lord. "The grass withereth, the flower fadeth, but the word of our God shall stand for ever." What a grand assurance! In life and in death we may rest our all, our immortal soul upon that firm foundation!

SERMON II.

THE UNVEILING OF SECRETS.

St. Luke xii. 2.—"For there is nothing covered, that shall not be revealed; neither hid, that shall not be known."

THERE is a solemn and a startling truth contained in these words. It is a truth that affects our private life, and touches the deepest depth of our heart. It tells us of a judgment to come.

In these days people try to ignore the fact that God has declared He will judge the earth. We find among men a tacit understanding not to say anything about it. Even Christians when they do venture to express an opinion, will oftentimes declare that the judgment is for the wicked and not for them. Yet the Scriptures emphatically state that "We shall all stand before the judgment seat of Christ." And whether men talk about it or not, the fact remains. If the Word of God be true, there comes a day in which every son and daughter of earth will stand before the great white throne of the Almighty.

In that day the secrets of all hearts shall be made known. Men and angels shall then see us, not as we seem to be, but as we actually are. Mysteries, to the solution of which we have now no clue, will then be as plain as the broad daylight. The soul will be unveiled and its hidden thoughts be openly manifested. "For there is nothing covered, that shall not be revealed; neither hid, that shall not be known."

There are many things hid from us now. Many a dark page of history is absolutely impenetrable to the keenest vision of the ablest criticism. Events that have startled the world are so covered up that we cannot tell anything concerning the causes that brought them about. Long periods of time are shrouded in a gloom that is rendered still deeper by the few solitary facts which have come down to us. And if this be true of events, the importance of which no words can estimate, is it not much more so of the great mass of individuals who have lived and died in the ages past? Not only are their deeds—whether good or bad—forgotten, but the men themselves are remembered no more; nay, we are not conscious that they ever existed. We know somebody must have lived in the centuries long ago, but that is all we know or can know at this time. Even our own ancestors have perished in this general oblivion. And as the individuals themselves have passed away from us, what of their sins—their words—their thoughts? If there can be degrees of impossibility, is it not in the very highest degree impossible for us to discover these? How can we ever grasp the secret thought of one who is to us absolutely unknown? But have those thoughts, those sins, those individuals, those hidden ages been lost for ever? Have they perished beneath the thick darkness that now envelopes them? Will the veil never be lifted? Shall we never see them: never know anything about them?

Our text answers the question. The day is coming when all shall be revealed. The day is coming when time shall be declared to be no more, and the long-forgotten past shall be one actual living present. We shall know the secrets of history, the secrets of individuals, the secrets of thoughts. The past of Assyria, of Egypt, of the world, will be plain. The lives of our ancestors will be opened unto all. The thoughts that the thinkers have forgotten will be remembered and made known to all men. This, I again repeat, is a solemn and startling fact. It is enough to fill us with fear and astonishment.

But we come down a little nearer home and we see that we ourselves will thus be revealed to others. The sins which we committed when we thought no one was nigh, the thoughts which we entertained that no one ever knew, are to be exhibited in living colours before the world. "Whatsoever," says Christ, "ye have spoken in darkness shall be heard in the light; and that which ye have spoken in the ear in closets shall be proclaimed upon the housetops."

We do not always think of this. Men say the darkness will hide them, the silence of night will not reveal their sin. There is always a tendency to forget or ignore the solemn truth that all will be manifested in the last great day. We know that in our day or land few men would commit gross sins on the open street in the broad daylight. We do not see a great deal of wickedness on the surface of society. The stream rolls along with only here and there a little fleck of scum floating past, which is however indicative of some disturbance in the depths beneath. We may not see the sin, but we know there is sin somewhere. It is not fashionable to sin publicly, and we may thank God that it is not, but for all that there are the secret sins. I do not say they take the same form or exist to the same extent in all. But they are there. A man in business sees the opportunity of obtaining an advantage over a customer; he thinks neither the customer nor any one else will ever know of it, and if he be not a conscientious man the step is taken. A servant may see no harm in wasting time or material when the employer is out of sight. A school-boy may think it is all right to peep into his book at an examination when the master is not looking. I do not believe every school-boy, servant or tradesman would do these things; far from it, but if they did them, it would be secretly with the idea that no one would ever know.

But these are small matters compared with others. Take the great sins of men. The forgerer puts the extra figures to the note or adds the signature to it with the belief that it will never be discovered. The burglar enters the house when he thinks no one will see him. The drunkard tries to conceal his crime like every other criminal. And need I point to the adulterer and the licentious sinner committing the sin of which it is not fitting to speak, and which they fondly hope may remain forever a secret?

Moreover do we not all know when sin has the greatest advantage over us? Is it not when we are alone—when no human eye is on us and we forget that God is there? There are temptations that have great power when we are in the company of evil men; but temptations that lead to the greatest sins have greatest power when we are away from all. The sin and wickedness that the corrupt and evil heart of man can evolve is amazing if not inconceivable. And when Satan meets us alone and suggests the fact that we are alone and that the sin we would commit may remain for ever unknown, it needs the greatest exercise of Divine grace to save us from falling.

I am speaking of fact. We have all sinned and we know what sin is. There is surely no one who may read these pages that has never felt the power of temptation. I will not say tempted to the same sin, for we have our individual temptations: but tempted so as to commit sin. We have committed sin—perhaps not what the world calls sin—yet sin both against God and against ourselves. We have entertained evil thoughts of others—we have murmured against God—we have had envy and bitterness in our heart. Even our acts of religion have been stained with sin. We have neglected duties that we ought to have done, and we have said that, perhaps from malice, perhaps from thoughtlessness, which was derogatory to our neighbour. There are a thousand ways in which we have sinned. But we have covered it all up. We have spread a thick veil over it. We have shrouded it with the shroud of forgetfulness. And we think it may remain thus forever. But the day comes when we shall learn the grand mistake. The secret sin will be known to all. The hidden thought will be told in every ear. We shall stand before an assembled world as we really are. In that day nothing will remain longer hid. Memory will have no shortcomings, it will be perfect, not able to forget. The past will be remembered, revealed, made known to all—the past of our lives, of mine, dear reader, and of yours!

How shall we stand then? How shall we feel when the night shall no longer cover us; when we shall be seen in all our sinfulness by friend, parent, brother, sister, wife, God? Think of it, for it is something that needs thinking of. We know it often happens in this life that the sin is discovered and made known. We see the blush of shame, the tremour of disgrace, possessing one thus discovered. We know of criminals when before the judge unable to lift up their head. We know of men— sinners against society—who walk our streets and wish that the great rocks might fall upon them and hide them from the gaze of men. But when we ourselves stand before God—when no witnesses of our guilt are needed—when we are our own accusers—when conscience has assumed its fullest power and brands us with the dark marks of guilt—how then? How shall we feel when the moments of sin are brought to mind and made known —when the sin that we thought was safely locked up in the bosom of the past is declared before the world, when the wrong we have done to another little dreamt of by him is told him in words of stern reality—oh, how shall we feel then? Will not the eye be downcast and the cheek flushed with confusion? Will not the body tremble and the tongue refuse to utter an excuse? Will not the burning sense of guilt rush through the brain leaving in its fiery track a caustic trail of deepest remorse, that shall bite and bite again till hell shall burn our very soul? Oh it is enough to make us tremble now! It is enough to send the throb of fear through every fibre of our being! It is enough to make us wish we had never been born—when we are told by the mouth of God Himself that "there is nothing covered, that shall not be revealed; neither hid that shall not be known."

I tremble as I ask again—how shall we stand in that great and terrible day?—you and I, preacher and reader, before the judgment seat of Christ?

Who knows how near the time may be when we may be called to give an account of our stewardship, an account of every idle word we may have spoken, an account of every sinful thought we may have entertained? And what account can we give? Is it not of sin, sin that overshadows every good deed we may have done? There we stand sinners against ourselves, our neighbours and our God, our soul robed in guilt, our inner life tainted with iniquity. What shall we do in that awful moment?

One thing is very certain, that criminals convicted of crime are not allowed to go scot-free. Our sins must be punished. This justice demands. How right this is reason tells us. We feel that retribution must come sometime, and as it does not come altogether in this life, it will in the life to come. How great then must be the punishment when sin after sin is brought to light! Can we ever expiate those sins? Can we ever redeem that life of evil? Will eternity itself be long enough to purge the soul of its iniquity and sin? It would seem impossible; nay, the Scriptures declare it to be so.

So that the fear of punishment will be added to the shame at the discovery of our sin. But no fear in its dire anticipations will exceed the bitterness of that shame. I can imagine the mute astonishment that will at first seize the guilty soul changing into a cry of mingled dread and reproach that will pierce the very welkin of heaven with its note of sharpened pain. I can imagine the cry rushing from mouth to mouth, from soul to soul, "Where can I hide me?" We shall want to hide somewhere then. We shall want some place where no one may see our shame-stricken face. We shall want to get out of the sight of that terrible gaze of men, of angels and of God.

I should be forgetful of the ministry of love were I not to depart from the direct point of my text and remind you, dear reader, of the refuge God has provided. It is the old, old story of God's love to man and of His desire to save him from sin and its sad consequences. The punishment of those sins has already been suffered, not by us but by another— even the Lord Jesus—in our stead. He has expiated every one of them, and if we will accept His atonement all is well. God has indeed a heavy bill against us but Jesus Christ has paid the bill and we are free. The object of the Gospel is to tell us these glad tidings. God asks us to accept our paid bill. How strange of us to try to pay it over twice! Yet this is just what we are endeavouring to do when we set aside Christ's work and attempt to work out our own redemption ourselves. God has laid upon Him the iniquity of us all.

You go into a merchant's office and looking over his old ledgers—ledgers that have long since been laid aside and are dusty with age—you may find accounts that your father, perhaps you yourself, contracted long ago. But they are all paid. Very likely a mark of red ink stretches from the top to the bottom of the page, crossing them out. Suppose you disputed the evidence of that red line. Suppose, when the merchant said to you, "the accounts are all settled—see this line is evidence enough for me," you were to reply, "I see it, but for all that I do not believe the debt is paid and I prefer paying it again," what could he do but accept your word? You will not acknowledge the fact, but are determined to pay the money. Yet this act of rare folly is what is done commonly and regularly in regard to spiritual matters. There are heavy accounts against us in God's book, but they are crossed out with the red line of the Saviour's blood. God tells us so. Shall we not believe Him? Shall we set aside that red mark and pay the bill ourselves again? Then surely as the Lord liveth we shall have no escape when we stand before the throne for judgment. We shall have to stand alone in our sins and pay by our eternal punishment the penalty we have ourselves incurred!

Surely the subject of which I am writing is a personal one. It concerns every one. It speaks to every heart. Two things are very sure: one is, that every secret will be made known; the other is, that for very shame we shall need some place where we may hide us from the gazing throng. We have such a hiding place in the Rock Christ Jesus. This is what the hymn means,

> " Rock of Ages, cleft for me,
> Let me hide myself in Thee."

We may hide in that Rock in the great day and no eye shall see our shame. As each revelation of our past is made we may plead the name of Jesus and all will be forgiven. There is a glorious hope that may cheer us when we think of what will hereafter be told of us. Is it our hope? Is it your hope, my brother, my sister, with which you expect to meet the trial of that day? Do you believe that the debt is paid, and that Jesus will be your refuge? Then though you may think of what is coming with shame because you have gone so far astray, yet you may thank God for having saved you. All will be well.

But do not think this gives us license to sin, or makes it a matter of indifference whether we sin or not. If we believe in Christ we are trying to serve Him—to serve Him by abstaining from all sin. It is the earnest desire of every true Christian to lead a new life. He remembers that in his secret moments God is with him. He remembers that when no other eye sees him God sees him. The Lord looks into his heart, and weighs his motives, and learns his thoughts. Nothing is hid from Him. And depend upon it, my dear reader, sin leaves its marks.

The fact that we have sinned must ever remain. The sin may be forgiven, but the fact cannot be destroyed. Its stain may be washed out so that no spot of guilt may be left, but the place where the stain has been will forever remind us of our past—will forever remind us of what we owe to Christ. We must bear all this in mind. We must not think we shall forever remain hid. The night that makes our soul a secret, a mystery to others, will not last forever. Our virtues and our vices, our good deeds and our bad, will be laid open in the bright light of the eternal day. Shall it be said of us at that time that we have obeyed God's commands and have believed in His Son, or shall only our sins appear with nothing to balance, nothing to offset them? It is for us to say now: "for there is nothing covered, that shall not be revealed; neither hid, that shall not be known."

SERMON III.

UNBELIEF.

St. Mark vi. 6.—" He marvelled because of their unbelief."

IF the Lord Jesus marvelled at the unbelief which greeted Him in His day, it is no wonder we should marvel at the unbelief which greets us in our day. That there is in the world at this present moment an immense amount of unbelief, none can deny. We can only wonder at it. We can only wonder that at this time when we have so much learning, so much ecclesiastical machinery, when Christianity has been vindicated so repeatedly by mighty champions, that it seems no longer possible to doubt, there still should be such an amazing spirit of infidelity in our midst. And what is even more saddening and depressing, is the fact that this spirit of scepticism has taken hold of the young men of our land like some fast spreading epidemic. The plague spot is everywhere. The flower of our youth is tainted with the foul leprosy.

And yet it is not always an active infidelity. On the contrary, it is generally a latent scepticism manifesting itself mainly in a profound indifference to religious truth. I do not think it is what might be called an intellectual scepticism, for that implies thought, and I do not think it can be safely said that the majority of our youth who are carried away by the specious arguments of infidels, give much thought to the subject. Nor do I think we can call it a grossly blasphemous scepticism. There may be some who would talk of religion in the spirit of a Tom Paine or a Voltaire, but the society of the day would rule them out at once. Our young men do not, perhaps, enter into the lists—they simply do not believe. They would ignore religion. They entertain ideas of it which would startle them were they expressed in bold, plain words.

This, however, is not true of all. While we find this latent scepticism in the mass, we see it developing through its various stages to active infidelity in others. A young man, proud like a newly fledged bird of his power of flight, delights to soar away upon the untried wings of his reason into heights that more experienced thinkers know are unsafe and dangerous. He sets aside all authority. First the Church goes, then the Bible goes, then natural religion goes, and up in the blue ether there he imagines there are no more rocks to bar his progress, nothing in his way, nothing above him, nothing beneath him. And when he finds the air growing thinner and thinner so that at last it is not able to bear him up, and his wings getting weaker and weaker so that he is continually fluttering and falling with broken flight, he begins to lose confidence in everything. He has been dabbling about where he was never intended to dabble, and he has lost faith in all. And when he comes down to earth again, it is only to carry on a bitter warfare against that very authority which he rejected and which he now thinks is responsible for all his trouble. He is an intellectual wreck. We have a great many of them about! They are the most pitiable cases of all. They are the sickly young men that have the finger of death upon them. They surround us on every hand.

Now, when a man sets aside all authority in the matter of religion, he has not far to go before he denies the existence of a God altogether. The probability is, that the very confusion of thought involved at this stage drives him hastily to a conclusion that at the first he had no idea of adopting. A want of cool, considerate thought makes him, like the fool, say in his heart, "There is no God." We have those who deny the truth of Christianity only, and those who deny all religion absolutely. One class arises from a too exalted idea of human reason; the other arises from not exercising reason enough, from a lack of thinking—the fool. David was right when he called him the fool. None but a fool could go so far as to say there is no God. And thus we have among our young men infidelity represented in the indifferent stage, in the lofty thinking stage, in the rejection of Christianity stage, till finally it reaches the stage of simple foolishness.

But at the bottom of it all is the one thing. It is but a germ at first, but it grows—and as we see it growing, as we see it making wrecks of the minds and bodies of our young men, as we see it leading them into sin (for infidelity and immorality are twin-brothers after all), pain fills our hearts. We are touched at the misery involved in the sad sight before us. A mingled feeling of pain and wonder seizes us. We would fain do something to arrest the further growth of this giant evil.

And in order to do this, I would touch briefly upon some of the causes that lead to this scepticism and suggest what remedies might be applied to remove them.

And first of all, we have the old cry against DOGMA. Christianity, our opponents say, is too dogmatical. But I do not believe this has anything to do with the question. The Church is not one whit more dogmatical than is the so-called Science of the day. Rationalists are quite as positive about their convictions as Theologians. For instance, Mr. Huxley says that "of the causes that led to the origination of living matter, we know absolutely nothing;" the Bible declares that God made everything. Both utterances are dogmatical. So I do not think it is mere dogma that does the mischief. But 1 do think it is done when dogma is advanced that cannot fairly be supported. There are rash statements of doctrine made. People, for want of culture and proper theological training, give false views of the truth and say things that they are not able to prove or that ought to be expressed in a very different manner. There is a surprising amount of bad theology rife. Let me give an illustration. We have the dogma advanced by some called Baptismal Regeneration. This doctrine claims that a little child, that can neither understand good nor evil, is changed *by Baptism* into a child of God. It is born again. Men of the world know such a dogma is false. It is not supported by facts. We have not a tittle of evidence to prove that such a change has taken place; most frequently we have every evidence to show it has not. Now dogmas advanced such as this—dogmas which are purely fictitious and have not an atom of proof to sustain them—lead directly to scepticism. You strenuously uphold an error of this kind and allow a man to doubt it, and ere long he will doubt everything else you say. And so, in my humble judgment, I hold that system of false dogmas known as Ritualism, responsible for a great deal of the infidelity of the day. That system presents to men that which their reason, if they think at all, tells them to be untrue. It combines fiction with fact, it mingles error with truth, and as the fiction and the error are discarded, the mind is prepared to question and doubt the fact and the truth. As a proof of this, I need only refer to what we see in lands where its sister creed has full sway. In

France, for instance, Infidelity and Romanism go hand in hand.

Moreover, when a dogma is attacked it must be well defended. It is no use to lay down a doctrine that we are not prepared to maintain, and that with such arguments as will commend themselves to reasonable people. We must either be able to base it upon sufficient authority, or discuss it with clearness and ability. If our arguments are weak and flimsy we induce scepticism. If a man perceives that we are weak on one point, he will get an idea that we are weak on some other point, and if he sees that some of our dogmas are without foundation, he will be very likely to question whether all our dogmas are not as equally without foundation. We, therefore, require care in stating the principles of Christian truth and power to defend them when assailed.

And so if we would remove this cause of infidelity, we must, as Christians, become better acquainted with the fundamentals of our faith. We must be well up in our Bibles. We must know something about articles and creeds. We must be able to give a reason for the faith that is in us. And those amongst us who have the time and ability, should verse themselves in the mighty arguments of such giants of Christianity as Butler, Paley, Pearson and others, whose writings have never been answered and would seem to be unanswerable. These old weapons have been tried and are worthy of being tried again. We have nothing like them now. The old is better than the new. And we can use them not merely upon the authority of those men of might, but upon their own intrinsic merit. And such as have neither time nor ability to study questions of this sort must be content to yield themselves to the inevitable and be submissive to the authority of men of superior power. We cannot all be Sir Isaac Newtons, or Lord Bacons, or Bishop Butlers. We must necessarily acquiesce in the conclusions arrived at by the leaders of thought. We must listen to authority. And to us, as Protestant Episcopalians, what better authority can we need than the simple, broad doctrinal declarations of our Scriptural Church, as embodied in the Thirty-nine Articles? Her decisions are the accumulated opinions of the wise men of all ages. And though I do not suppose for one moment that her decrees will have any weight with unbelievers, yet we can entrench ourselves behind her authority and present to our opponents so bold a front that they cannot but feel shaken in their determination. Standing upon the simple utterances of our Church, we can dare them to remove them before we yield for an instant our own cherished principles.

But we have a cause leading to scepticism still more powerful than our groundless assertions or weak arguments. These only touch certain classes of people. The one I am about to mention has an immense influence over all. IT IS THE FALSE PROfessions of Christians. There are large numbers of men and women claiming the name of Christian, who are Christians only in name. They are not Christians in fact. They do not live out what they say they believe. They are very like a man who in times of war declares himself to be a loyal citizen of one country and yet goes and fights against it with its enemies. These people do our cause an immense amount of damage. It is harmful to see a Christian do acts which his profession condemns as evil. Nothing is more common than for young men of the world, when called upon to lead a holy life, to refer to the numberless instances of individuals who have disgraced their calling. A bishop is deposed for immorality, a clergyman is degraded for fraudulent transactions, a leading member of the Church, a Sunday School teacher, is convicted of crime—and they are pointed at as specimens of Christian profession. It is no use to say these are the exceptions, not the rule. People of the world will not look at anything but the exceptions. When some strange meteor flashes across the sky men look at it and talk about it, and forget for the time, the stars shining so regularly and quietly around it. And it is not only these great irregularities that are pointed to, but the general inconsistencies of Christians. There is, we must all admit, a great spirit of worldliness in the Church at this time. The people of God live so close in their habits to the people of the world that it is hard to distinguish them. One is inclined to ask what is the difference between them? When we profess to believe in a God rendering justice to every man, in a judgment to come, in a state of rewards and punishments, and live as though we regarded these things as of no consequence, we cannot but lead a man to suppose that we do not actually believe in them. And so he will justify himself in disbelieving them. He will cast them on one side. And this we find is really the case. Hundreds of young men are ruined through the evil example of insincerity set them by others.

And depend upon it, if we would strike an effective blow at the evil which surrounds us, it must be by a better and manlier Christianity. There must be a reality about what we profess. It is no use to say one thing and do another. It is no use to tell a man we are walking in the path of life when we are sitting in the seat of sin. Let us be up and doing. Let us show the world that the profession we make with our lips is indeed the profession of our heart. Let us show every one that we are coolly and calmly but none the less truly dead in earnest. In all our life let Christianity be first. And then when our unbelieving friends see that by our actions we express our faith, they may be inclined to think that there is something in that faith. We shall certainly not drive them away, and we may attract them to us.

But besides this insincerity we have another cause closely analogous to it, and that is A LACK OF ZEAL ON THE PART OF CHRISTIANS. We have zeal enough of a certain sort. We have zeal enough on the part of many to set aside every institution be it ever so divine. We have zeal enough on the part of some truly good people to ignore the Church and substitute some human organization in its place. But of the zeal that shall manifest itself in an honest simple desire to save men's souls, of the zeal that shall forget self and go out in the name of the Master to the lost and ruined and bring them into God's fold, the Church, we have not enough. I know not how it is. It cannot surely be from a fear of interfering with the work and duty of the ministry. No simple evangelization can interfere with the office of that sacred order. No evangelist takes upon himself the authority which is given exclusively to those appointed overseers in the House of God. They do not usurp the right of government, or administration of sacraments, or authoritatively pronounce decrees of doctrine. When they feel called upon to do this much they enter the ministry itself. But there is immense work open for laymen to engage in outside of all this. They have the right and it is their duty to try to save men's souls whenever they are able. The work of simply declaring the glad tidings of the Gospel is not confined to the ministry. I remember when I was in Port Hope a train on the Midland Railway became utterly unmanageable. It tore along the road at a fearful rate. Trees, bridges and stations were passed with a speed growing greater all the time. At last it dashed into the town and in all its fury with its living freight on board rushed on towards the lake. A few minutes and the whole train would have reached the wharf, and in an instant a catastrophe awful to think of would have taken place. There is, however, at a little distance from the wharf a branch line with an up grade connecting the Midland Road with the Grand Trunk. If the switch were turned the train might be saved. It so happened a young man passing by at the time seeing the train towering along thought of this, and in an instant rushed to the switch, and in another instant the train was diverted from its course of death, and having an upgrade to contend with soon became manageable. It was not the office of that young man to attend to that switch. He was not set apart for it. There was no one else near that was set apart for it, but right or wrong he did it, and many lives were thereby saved. Depend upon it there are souls around us that are rushing on to death, as was that train, only to a death more fearful. Shall they be allowed to go on because the proper official is not on hand to turn the switch? Shall we do nothing because we have not been specially allotted to that task? Away with such a mischievous, murderous policy! Let us recognize it to be the duty of every man to save another man's soul as he would his life could he get the chance. If we were to do this it would help us marvellously in our strife with infidelity. When men see us standing by the switch and doing nothing to save the train rushing on to destruction, they will never believe in our professions of love for humanity. And when they see a whole host of professing Christians doing nothing whatever to save their friends and their neighbours from the death of deaths, they will say we care nothing for them; that our religion is an empty show; that it is verily untrue. Thus by a lack of zeal we induce scepticism. We become ourselves responsible for a great deal of the infidelity of the day.

I mention these three causes because I think they can be practically dealt with. I have said enough in a simple way to show what we can all of us do in our sphere to stem the tide. Others have gone into the subject more elaborately. But let these few suggestions be carried out—and they are but common-place truths—and something will actually have been done to save our brethren from their sad condition. Be yourself, dear reader, simple and plain in what you say about religion; let it be on authority. Be sincere; live your religion out. Be zealous—zealous to save souls. And thus you may help most efficiently in this great work. And do not think there is nothing that can be done. All can do something. Do you not believe it? The Lord Jesus would marvel at such unbelief. Depend upon it a faith without works is dead—it is practically unbelief. Can we expect others to believe if we do not believe ourselves? The point of our text is turned from what we see abroad to our own hearts. We may rather marvel at the unbelief we see there. After all our privileges we should yet remain in practical infidelity! Oh let us change this sort of thing! Let us rouse ourselves in our might! Christian reader, think of what you can do for others by your example, and remember that God expects us all to do our duty.

We live in an age peculiar in its mode of thought. It is an age of indifference and faithlessness. There is no great originality of thought but an intense criticism. I do not fear this. I believe Christianity after the conflict of nineteen centuries can hold its own through the battle of the coming generations. But I fear the effects of all this on the men of our own day. A writer the other day told us in painfully vivid words: "It is said that in tropical forests one can almost hear the vegetation growing. One may almost say that with us one can hear faith decaying." Fancy that! Standing in the forest of human life we may even hear the sad decay of faith, the withering leaves, the cracking bark, the falling timbers—the terrible approach of death.

Men are dying all around us because they have no faith—they cannot believe in the reality of religion. They are all the time seeking for a sign. They cry out for a proof. They want some evidence. Oh, let us by our lives, our words, our actions, give them the sign, the proof, the evidence. Let us show them that there is a reality in our religion. That it has a power in it to keep us from sin, to comfort us in sorrow, to make us strive to save our brethren. Let us step into the midst of the decaying forest and proclaim a living life. If they will not believe in that life let them at least see that we live. We shall then be free from their blood. We may then justly marvel at their unbelief. We may leave them in the hands of a God who, while just in all He does, is yet full of compassion and mercy.

And should there be any one who may read this whose mind has been disturbed by infidel arguments I can only ask him in all fairness to hear the other side. What Christianity is can be fully known only by trial. It says to all: "Come and see ; try me." Was such a trial ever made in vain ? No man has a right to reject Christianity until he has tried it, or at least until he can point to others who have tried it and failed to be convinced. I ask you honestly and seriously to give it a trial, and I am sure the result will be satisfaction to your own soul, a sweet calm of peace after the great storm of doubt.

May God give us all of the abundance of His

grace, that we may live as becomes the Gospel; that we may exalt our Saviour Christ wherever we are, in our words and in our life; and that all that we do may be in accordance with His will, and resting upon the authority of His word, so that at the last we may be received as faithful servants into the reward that God has promised to those who are faithful unto death!

SERMON IV.

THE MARVELLOUS CHANGE.

2 Corinthians III. 18.—"We all, with open face beholding as in a glass the glory of the Lord, are changed into the same image from glory to glory."

THE Apostle is speaking only of Believers. None but those whose eyes have been opened may behold the glory of the Lord. Christ has no attraction for the worldly and the ungodly. By them "He is despised and rejected." But His own people love to look upon Him—to them He is the chiefest among ten thousand and the altogether lovely. They have but the one wish to get nearer and still nearer to Him, to be folded in His arms, to lean like the beloved disciple upon the bosom of His love. The world without Him is all darkness, for He is their Sun and their Light; their path without Him is the path of death, for He alone is their Life; their future without Him is a blank, for He is their only Hope. He is therefore their All-and-in-all, their Alpha and Omega, their first and their last. They all with open face behold as in a glass the glory of their Lord.

The glass here spoken of is the blessed Gospel. There as in a mirror our Master is reflected all radiant in His glory. We read of Him in the beauty of His character, His work and His love;

and the more we read of Him the more we delight to linger upon those holy pages. Day after day we see something new there, some glory never before noticed, and things that once were dark are now light, for we behold them with open face. The veil of unbelief is removed and with a clear faith we see the reflection of our Lord in that book of books. And what is the result of this peering into the Gospel glass? what the effect? Our text tells us: "We are changed into the same image from glory to glory." We are made like Him. We partake of His spirit. His life, His purity, His obedience are implanted in our hearts. The glory which is displayed in that mirror is reflected back on us till we are bathed as it were in the refulgent light.

In this sermon I shall endeavour with God's blessing to draw the attention of my readers especially to this great change which is wrought in us by the steadfast gazing upon the Lord—a change, the Apostle tells us, which comes over all who look upon His glory.

And the *first thing* we may notice of it is, that it is a GRADUAL CHANGE.

It is "from glory to glory." The glory which we receive to-day develops into a greater glory to-morrow. It is not a sudden transformation. It is little by little, step by step, day by day. This is a very important point to remember. We have its parallel in every day life. Neither our minds nor our bodies leap at one bound from infancy to maturity. They grow gradually, slowly develop. A boy takes up the work of some great master of thought. He does not at once grasp the fulness of the ideas contained therein. It is only after long continued and persistent reading and thought the work becomes his own; and then he will find that his mind has been affected and moulded by the mind of his author, and this so gradually as at the time to be unnoticed. So it is in the young Christian studying the Gospel. He does not at first take it in in all its fulness. He does not behold all its beauties and glories at one glance. The undercurrent of living water will long lie hid beneath the surface-soil of difficulties; the nuggets of fine gold will long be out of sight amid the rocks of prejudice; but the more he reads the more he will behold Christ in those living waters, the more he will learn of heavenly things, the more his mind will be moulded into the image of the Master's mind. It is a gradual growth in grace. It is a gradual increase in glory.

Early in the morning we stand on a spur of a high mountain. At our feet is a broad, deep valley. Around us are other mountains raising aloft their pinnacled heights. All is silent darkness. Presently the gray clouds of the east are lighted up with the rays of the coming sun. Slowly they stretch across the sky till at last the highest points of the mountains are touched with the golden light. Little by little the gloom in the valley is reached, gradually the mists roll away, each minute brings the line of glory lower and lower down the mountain side, till at last every tree, brook, village and glen is flooded with the rich, bright sunshine. That which an hour or two before was hid in darkness is gradually changed till now we see it all in a glow of beauty. Very much so is it with us. When within us the Sun of Righteousness first arises the prominent points of our character are touched, but little by little the bright rays penetrate into the deep depths of our heart and drive away from them the cold, dark night. So when the germ of eternal life is imparted to our soul by the power of the Holy Ghost we commence to grow. At first we are verily babes, but day by day we become stronger and stronger—sin, which at first held us bound as it were, is resisted and conquered, powers which at one time were used in Satan's service, are consecrated to the worship and service of God, and we are gradually transformed into the image of the glory of the Lord. This follows as an inevitable result of true conversion. The glory which at first crowns the mountain tops ere long floods every thought, word and deed of the sincere believer.

And it is indeed a delightful thing to see this gradual change in Christian people. Living in the Lord they await the sanctification of His Spirit.

With open face—with earnest and growing faith—they peer into the deep things of the Gospel. We almost see the glory reflected back on them. We see devotion in the worship of God, obedience to His commands, resignation to His will, faith, love, and peace—growing greater and stronger all the time. We see the glory of the Lord in their life, their character, their work. It rests upon them like some crown of light, each gem growing brighter and brighter as it is touched with the Divine splendour. Then we know

" Old friends, old scenes will lovelier be,
As more of heaven in each we see."

We shall behold them changing from glory to glory. Beautiful in the bud, more beautiful in the flower, and still more beautiful in the fruit. Looking upon Christ, they become more Christ-like; His spirit shines in them; His glory is reflected upon them.

Such a change steals over all that come within its influence. It melts the cold icy heart, it developes the tender germ of life, it leads us on step by step to God. Oh that this change might be wrought in every reader of these sermons. Are we conscious that we have grown since we have believed? Is our faith stronger, our obedience more ready, our daily walk more holy? Are the rays of glory which are tinging the lofty heights coming down into the valley of our heart, so that not only the great things but the little things of our character are being touched with the Spirit of the Master? We may not note the daily change, but we can discern the change from year to year. Is this gradual change taking place in us?

But in the *second place* the change spoken of in our text is a PARTIAL CHANGE.

It is indeed very great—from glory to glory, but the fulness of glory cannot be ours in this life. Absolute perfection is reserved for the other world. " Beloved, now are we the sons of God, and it doth not yet appear what we shall be; but we know that when He shall appear, we shall be like Him; for we shall see Him as He is." Now we see but the reflection of Him in a glass. It is but an image; not the reality. "Now we see through a glass darkly; but then—in the hereafter—face to face: now I know in part; but then shall I know even as I am known." Every Christian must be indeed painfully conscious of this partial transformation. Our lives are so far from what we know they ought to be. After all our endeavours to follow in the footsteps of the Master we are yet so unlike Him. We have not that implicit obedience to the will of the Father, that earnest, child-like faith, that simple steady purpose, which formed the glory of His life while here on earth. We behold in the Gospel His self-denying love and His unwearying devotion; we are touched with His unchanging meekness, and His quiet, impressive dignity; we know that the perfection of holiness filled His very soul, and went out into all His words and works—and though the contemplation of all this cannot fail to have its effect upon us, yet we must feel after all how very far from Him we are—even the very best of us. We have an illustration of this in the great and good St. Paul. He was one that lived in the very odour of sanctity, and yet he was not perfect. When about to set out on one of his missionary tours, he disputed with Barnabas concerning "John, whose surname was Mark." "And the contention was so sharp between them that they departed asunder one from the other." We never have an instance of such anger in the Lord Jesus. It is interesting to notice how in after years St. Paul changed his mind over that very Mark. Writing to the Colossians he bids them "if he come unto you, receive him;" and writing to Timothy he says: "Take Mark and bring him with thee; for he is profitable to me for the ministry." I cannot but think that Paul must have sorrowed many times over his quarrel concerning a young man that proved after all to be a very useful minister. But Christ never does an action, or drops a word that implies any, the slightest trace, of a personal remorse. He is absolute perfection. His "severe and stainless beauty casts the shadow of failure upon all that is not Himself." The light we receive from the reflection of His image serves to show us how full of sin we are, and how partially changed into the image of the Master.

But, in that other world, the perfection which we see in Jesus will be in us. We shall be like Him. There will be no blemishes, no dark spots; all will be purity and glory. This quick temper, burning up so many resolutions, will be quenched for ever then. This murmuring spirit, making life so unhappy, these doubts and fears, retarding us in our heavenward progress, these besetting sins holding us in bondage, will all be gone then—gone for ever. What it will be, when we are absolutely changed, we cannot conceive. "Eye hath not seen, nor ear heard, neither have entered into the heart of man the things which God hath prepared for them that love Him;" for "the light of the moon shall be as the light of the sun, and the light of the sun shall be sevenfold, as the light of seven days, in the day that the Lord bindeth up the breach of his people and healeth the stroke of their wound." We shall stand before "the great white throne" and the countenance of Him who sits thereon shall be "as the sun shining in his strength," and we shall be changed into the like image and glory. Moses talked with God in the mount; but it was in the thick cloud and terrible darkness; yet, when he came down, the people were afraid to come nigh him; for his face shone with imparted glory. What then must be the glory of those who shall stand in His presence for ever and see Him face to face? Yet all this glory shall be ours when we behold our risen Lord sitting at the right hand of the Majesty on high. Here below we pass on from glory to glory. We are continually approaching perfection. We are changing, day by day, into the image of the Master. There is a flower, the blossom of which, when it first appears, is a plain white; but exposure to the sun gradually tints it with pink, and day after day, the pink darkens till it becomes a rich crimson and then it dies. So we in reading the Gospel are gradually tinged with glory; but it is an imperfect, a partial glory. When we have reached the fullest glory, we can bear in this life, we die and are transplanted to another world. It is a great thing to be under the influence of this change. Partial though it is, it is very much to be desired. It is a preparation for the fuller change beyond the grave. We should, therefore, turn our eyes upon the Lord and fix our gaze there; for "we all, with open face beholding, as in a glass, the glory of the Lord, are changed into the same image from glory to glory."

But, in the *third place*, the change the apostle is speaking of is a DIVINE CHANGE.

It is a change wrought entirely by God; the very glory we receive is His. On a bright, frosty day, when the sun shines from a clear Canadian sky upon a plain of white frozen snow, each crystal, exposed to the rays, will sparkle with glory. Yet we know, that were it not for the sun, all that dazzling splendour would be gloom and darkness. So man, sanctified by the Spirit, is glorious indeed to behold ; but it is not his glory only the reflection of God's. Take the glory of the Lord away and our hearts and lives are cold and dead. We have no glory of our own. We may light a bonfire, nay, set a whole forest on fire ; but what is that compared to the sun ? So we may lead a moral life ; but what is the glory of such a life when placed side by side with the glory of Christ's life, or with the reflected glory which belongs to His people ? When we see a man shewing, by his life and conversation, that he is, indeed, a child of God, we know that the change wrought in that man is a Divine change ; we know that he is reflecting the Master in his ways and work ; we know that the glory we see in him belongs to the Lord. And the effect of this is, we know that it will never die. What a wonderful thought !

" We are changed from glory to glory," by the Spirit of the Lord. All that God does for the souls of His people is eternal. God's glory cannot end. It will shine for ever and for ever. We shall be kept within its influence. Therefore the glory we shall have will never fade. It cannot because it is Divine. The clouds of despondency, that at one time may seem to shroud us in darkness, will pass away ;

the storms of temptation, that threaten to destroy us for ever, will come to an end ; the night of despair shall melt into the morn of joy, because the change is Divine.

There are some men whom the world delights to honour. They are men whom it is an honour to know and a still greater honour to serve. The honour, which is given to them, goes out to all around them. The glory, which a Nelson gained at Trafalgar, or a Wellington at Waterloo, is reflected upon the noble men who fought under them in those great battles. The glory centred in the general ; but it shines upon every man connected with him. They all profit by his skill, they all win renown by his bravery, they all share in his fame. So it is with those associated with the Lord Jesus. It is a greater honour than this world can give, to be permitted to fight under His standard. The glory which shall be His when all His enemies shall be put under His feet, when death itself shall be destroyed, shall go out and shine upon all those who bear His name, who have fought with Him against sin, and who own Him as their Lord and Master. But it will be His glory then in the day of victory ; it will be His might, His wisdom, His life that will be triumphant on the field of battle. And, so now in this life, when we peer into the gospel-glass, it is the glory of the Lord we see there. Every page is brilliant with His image. Every letter is radiant with His beauty,

And it is His glory, His image, His beauty which is reflected back to us, and into which we are changed. Take Christ out of the Bible and you have nothing left, that can make any impression on us. Take His image out of the glass, and we have a sky without a sun, a world without a day, a universe without its light.

And as the glory is Divine, it follows as a consequence, that the change we undergo is also Divine. If we place a plant in a dark room it will lose colour and vigour and form; but bring it out into the sunshine and ere long a marvellous change will take place. So place a man where he cannot see the glory of the Lord—that is to say, take him away from his Bible and the opportunity of hearing the Word, and he will grow weakly, sickly and death-like. But bring him out where he can look with open face into the glass, and the glory which he sees there will work a change in him—a change that will make him strong and healthy and full of life. It is a divine change—a change wrought even by the Spirit of the Lord!

As our thoughts dwell upon this wonderful change, surely some solemn and important questions must present themselves to us. And first of all we may ask ourselves; are we looking into the glass, are we beholding the glory of the Lord as contained in the pages of His gospel? We cannot expect to be made like Him if we are not.

We cannot expect to learn of Christ if we never read the story of His life and revelation. If we would grow in grace, if we would lead holy lives, if we would become Christ-like—we must read and study our Bible, we must make its sublime truths our own, we must live in the sunshine of our Master's glory. We see people who are sincerely desirous of living the new life ; they are trusting to God's mercy, they are convinced of sin, they long to get nearer to God, but they do not ; they are still far away,—and the secret of it is in the fact that they do not prayerfully and faithfully look upon Christ in the gospel-glass. There is not enough Bible reading in our day, and until there is we cannot expect to find an abundance of noble, manly, God-like Christians. Let us see to it that we do not neglect this solemn and all-important duty.

Perhaps, however, we do regularly read our Bibles and yet are conscious of no change taking place in us, and then we ask ourselves are we reading it aright ? There is a way of reading the Bible that does not advance our spiritual life. We may read it for simple curiosity or idle amusement. We may read it with the veil still upon our hearts. The only remedy in such a case is prayer—prayer that God may remove the veil—prayer that with open face we may behold the glory of the Lord. And this is what we always want with the reading of the Word. If God opens our eyes there will be no mistake about our seeing the truth, and if we see it, it will have its effect upon us. I do not say we shall be conscious of the change at the time—for it is a *gradual* change —a slow development of life. Nor do I say it will be a full, complete change—it is but *partial*, absolute perfection is in the other world. But I do say it will be *Divine*—we shall receive of the glory of Christ—we shall be made like unto Him. There can be no mistake about this. Prayer for sight and using that sight will have a good result. Reading of Christ, hearing of Christ, and thinking of Christ will work in us a glorious change—*gradually, partially* now, *perfectly* hereafter, *Divinely* for all time and for all eternity. For "we all with open face beholding as in a glass the glory of the Lord, are changed into the same image from glory to glory."

SERMON V.

APPEARING WITH CHRIST.

COLOSSIANS III. 4.—When Christ, who is our life, shall appear, then shall ye also appear with Him in glory.

THE lessons contained in our text are many and of deep importance. They are addressed to us for our comfort and edification. They shew us privileges and give us hopes that may cheer us in our sorrows and encourage us in our difficulties. The verse is, as it were, one of those brilliant gems in the book of light that shine out more prominently than the rest, and sparkle with a beauty and lustre that the dulness of earth cannot tarnish. Could anything be grander than this golden text: "When Christ, who is our life, shall appear, then shall ye also appear with Him in glory." Let us look at some of the truths it suggests.

And one of these is the blessed fact, stated to us again and again, of the INSEPARABLE CONNECTION BETWEEN CHRIST AND HIS PEOPLE.

When He shall appear we shall appear with Him. He cannot enter into His kingdom but we, His chosen ones, will enter in with Him. We are one with Him. The Scriptures continually set this truth before us. Our relationship to Christ is compared to that of a body of which He is the head and we the members. Belonging to the same individual organization, we must have the same ultimate destiny. If the head, which is Christ, enters into glory, then we, who are the members, will also enter into the same glory. In another place Christ compares Himself to a vine, of which we are the branches—so linked with Him that the one spirit pervades and runs through the whole. Hence the apostle says, " He that is joined to the Lord is one spirit." Again we are spoken of as a family—the family of God—in which Christ is our elder brother, only He is the one that sticketh closer than a brother. These strong figures are confirmed by many positive statements. Our blessed Lord declared to His sorrowing disciples: " If I go and prepare a place for you, I will come again and receive you unto myself, that where I am, there ye may be also." So He prays to His Father concerning His people that " they all may be one; as Thou, Father, art in Me, and I in Thee, that they also may be one in Us ;" and again He prays : " Father, I will that they also, whom Thou hast given Me, be with Me where I am." The apostles never lose sight of this important doctrine. '' There is now no condemnation to them which are in Christ Jesus," because He is free from all condemnation, and we are in Him. We are buried with Christ in baptism. We are raised with Christ in His resurrection. We shall sit down with Christ at the glorious marriage supper spoken of in the Revelation.

But all these figures and declarations are summed up in the brief sentence of our text. There the apostle states that Christ is our life. As in the body and the vine, the one life flows through it all, sustaining and invigorating it, so the one life—eternal life—which is in Christ, is the life of our souls—the first principle of all our actions. He is the bread of life—our heavenly food. Spiritually and by faith we feed upon His flesh and blood. Thus we are incorporated with Him. Thus we live and move in Him and have our being. There can be no separation of us from Him without injury to the whole.

The comfort this blessed truth can give is inestimable. Many a poor trembling, tempest-tossed soul is sustained in its weakness and distress by the thought that it is Christ's. There are no terrors that Satan may threaten us with, no sorrows that an envious world may cause us, that can possibly overwhelm us in utter despair so long as we have such a foundation truth as this to rest upon. We may be secure on this rock. We may bid defiance to the wildest storm. We may stand undaunted at the roar and fury of the mighty breaking billows. Temptations may assault us; tribulation may almost rend our heart; sin may cast us level with the dust, but they cannot prevail. We are Christ's. Whether we live or whether we die we are the Lord's. In the day of prosperity or in the day of adversity still there is no change—the God of Israel changeth not, and those who are His shall never perish. What a glorious hope for the Christian! Well might good old Rowland Hill sing on his dying bed:

"And when I'm to die, 'Receive me' I'll cry,
For Jesus hath loved me, I cannot tell why;
But this I do find—we two are so joined,
He'll not be in heaven and leave me behind."

No! "Even when we were dead in sins, God quickened us together with Christ, and hath raised us up together and made us sit together in heavenly places in Christ Jesus." This is the lesson taught us in our text. We are inseparably connected with Christ. And as we are thus intimately joined with Him, so is He necessarily as intimately joined with us. Our trials are His trials. Our sorrows are His sorrows. Our shame is His shame. We cannot suffer but He suffers with us. He makes the tribulations of His people His own. When He met Saul, the persecutor, on the way to Damascus, it was not "Saul, Saul, why persecutest thou My people?" but "Saul, Saul, why persecutest thou Me?" To touch one of the least of His followers was to touch Him. The pain inflicted on one member of the body thrills through the whole and is felt by the life. And so when we are in distress we may rejoice, yea even though we are passing through the valley of the shadow of death, at the remembrance that He, our Master, feels our sufferings, and bears with us our cross. Death has no sting in such a case. Our life is hid with Christ in God. He is our life.

A *second* lesson we find taught in our text is the important doctrine of CHRIST'S SECOND ADVENT.

" When Christ, who is our life, shall appear "—He is to appear to the world again. " This same Jesus, which is taken up from you into heaven, shall so come in like manner as ye have seen Him go into Heaven." All the tribes of the earth " shall see the Son of Man coming in the clouds of heaven with power and great glory." It is not to be a coming that no one knows anything about, but a real, literal manifestation—a coming in which " every eye shall see Him, and they also which pierced Him ; and all kindreds of the earth shall wail because of him." This is a truth that we are oftentimes very slow of heart to believe. We are too apt to look upon the prophecies of Scriptures which are yet unfulfilled as merely figurative, and yet there is not a single prophecy which has been fulfilled that was not fulfilled literally and to the letter. When Isaiah foretold the coming of the Messiah, he pointed to no figurative coming and to no figurative Christ, but to an actual, visible advent, to an actual, visible Saviour. And depend upon it there are not two rules for interpreting prophecies of this kind. The second advent is to be just as real and just as visible as the first. The

Lord Jesus will appear to men in that great day as actually and verily as he appeared to the men in Jerusalem eighteen hundred years ago. If the Word of God relating to this doctrine is not to be taken literally and as it stands, then everything else affirmed in that blessed book loses its reality and becomes a myth. Salvation is a myth. Eternal life is a myth. Heaven is a myth. Nay, even God Himself and the person and work of Christ are nothing else but myths. There is no reality—no substance in any of the gracious promises of our Father. Everything may be reasoned away and made to appear as an idle dream. I cannot believe such a theory of interpretation as that. I see the Scriptures fulfilled literally in everything else and I believe they will be in this. I believe that Christ will appear again as our text declares, and that we shall see Him —the just and the unjust, the saint and the sinner, and shall stand before His throne for judgment, and receive the just reward or the just punishment for the deeds done in the flesh. And I believe, too, that though there will be signs in the sun and in the moon, though there will be wonderful manifestations both in Heaven and on earth, yet men will refuse to read them, will refuse to notice them, and while they are marrying and giving in marriage, living as though there were to be no end, the day of the Lord will come upon them suddenly and unexpectedly as a thief in the night. In the midst of their careless slumber, nature will be convulsed, the clouds will be rent in sunder, and, as the Scripture says, "the Lord Himself shall descend from Heaven with a shout, with the voice of the archangel and with the trump of God." And the voice, and the shout, and the trump of His coming shall resound across earth's lands and seas, waking the dead and arousing the living, and calling them both to judgment. Then we, who are Christ's and are alive at His coming, shall wait until the dead in Christ are raised, and then together with them will be caught up in the clouds to meet the Lord in the air, while those who are left behind on the ground—the wicked and reprobate—will hide themselves in the dens and in the rocks of the mountains, and will say to the mountains and the rocks, "Fall on us, and hide us from the face of Him that sitteth on the throne, and from the wrath of the Lamb; for the great day of His wrath is come, and who shall be able to stand?"

This glorious and yet terrible appearing our text brings to our notice. We are looking forward to it as our fathers did. Year by year our attention is specially directed to this final consummation of all things, to the commencement of the eternal dispensation, of the new heavens and the new earth "wherein dwelleth righteousness." With longing hearts we would see Jesus. We would see Him in His glory. We would see Him face to face as the disciples of olden time saw Him. We would see

Him surrounded with His ransomed Israel reigning as the King of kings in the city of the New Jerusalem. And though "since the fathers fell asleep, all things continue as they were from the beginning of the creation," yet we know "the Lord is not slack concerning His promise," "for we shall see Him as He is." We shall behold with opened eye the Bright and Morning Star; the Salvation of the daughter of Zion; the Author and Finisher of our Faith; the Redeemer of the World. More than this we shall see Him as the One who is our life; as the One with whom our souls, our past, our future, our all, are inseparably connected. As Christians we may then, when we think of what He is to us, look forward to His coming with joy. It is our great hope, our eternal glory. There is nothing to fill us with fear or to make us doubt the truth I am now proclaiming. We are His; bought with the price of His most precious blood, saved by the offering up of the sacrifice of Himself: that is sufficient. And the text before us declares as plainly as words can declare a thing, that He shall appear, He shall come again.

But the *third* lesson we are taught is that "when Christ, who is our life, shall appear, THEN SHALL WE ALSO APPEAR WITH HIM IN GLORY." A statement concerning our own destiny is given us. Our ultimate reward is set before us.

We all know that in this life shame is our portion. Kindly disposed as the professing Church and the world seem to be towards each other there is still much shame attached to the true child of God. The religion of the Lord Jesus and the religion of unregenerate man are as much opposed to one another to-day as they were in the days of old. Nor can we be real Christians without being despised of men. The world will indeed speak kindly of us so long as we say nothing of its sins and are not too outspoken in our convictions. But the moment we stand up for the truth as it is in Jesus, the moment we separate ourselves from the company of the ungodly and refuse to associate with them, then the world's tone towards us changes. It expresses its hatred for us in calling us hard names, in sharp, cutting sneers, in deep, bitter, relentless persecution. Just as it hated Christ when He was on earth, so it hates His people now. We must expect this; the servant is not above his Lord. The conflict and the hatred will last as long as the world stands. True religion will ever be a thorn in the side of unbelief. Irreligious men and women will ever despise those who are trying to keep themselves unspotted from the world. Our path will be a path of shame as was our Master's path. We must bear the cross, yea though we faint beneath its weight. And all this shame will last " till He come." But " when Christ who is our life shall appear, then shall we also appear with

E

Him in glory." At His advent all will be changed. We shall no longer be despised and rejected of men, but princes in the Kingdom of God, lords over worlds and angels. We shall no longer labour under the cross, but wear the crown—the crown of righteousness which the Lord the righteous Judge will give unto all that love His appearing. There will be exaltation and honour and glory such as no tongue can express. "Eye hath not seen nor ear heard, neither have entered into the heart of man, the things which God hath prepared for them that love Him." "Now are we the sons of God; and it doth not yet appear what we shall be: but we know that when He shall appear we shall be like Him, for we shall see Him as He is." Moses was in the mountain alone with God, but he saw not the fulness of His glory, for the thick cloud hid Him, yet the few rays of divine majesty that touched him made his face so to shine that men could not look upon him. How glorious then shall they be who through the rent veil with sanctified hearts shall behold in all His fulness the King of Glory, the God-crowned Saviour of men! Verily they shall be transfigured into a like glory. We shall be like Him. And just as Peter and James and John fell down and hid their faces when they saw their Lord with Moses and Elias in their heavenly glory, so shall the ungodly in the great day tremble and fear when they see our glory—the glory of our life, the glory of Him who is the light of the eternal city, before whose majesty the radiance of ten thousand suns pales and fades away. There will be no more shame for us then. There will be no more sneers, no more taunts, no more persecutions. All will be over then. We shall enter in with Him into the home of the blessed where we shall see His face, and where His name shall be in our foreheads. Our glorified bodies made like unto His glorious body shall forever be freed from sickness, sorrow and death. Our ransomed souls, free from sin, and pure as He is pure, shall forever sing the new song which none but the redeemed of earth can sing. This will be glory. Whatever the Lord Jesus is, we shall be. When He shall reign we shall also reign. When He shall be exalted we shall also be exalted. We are one with Him. He is our very life. And when He shall appear, whether it be to men, to angels, or to God, we shall also appear with Him in glory. This is our reward. This is the destiny that shall be attained by all the children of God.

Beloved reader, we do well to look forward to the day of His coming. We are to watch for it and to wait for it as those who love His appearing. Our text teaches us that we are His. It tells us that He will certainly come again. It declares that when he does come we shall indeed be like Him. What glorious news is all this! How it makes the heart thrill with joy! Yet we feel how unworthy we are of it all. Why should we receive such great glory? What have we done, what can we do, to merit such a blessed relationship, to be saved with such a wonderful salvation! We have done nothing: nay can do nothing!

> "Nothing, sinner, great or small,
> Nothing, sinner, no :
> Jesus died and did it all
> Long, long ago."

It is simply and solely because Christ died that we live. It is simply and solely because Christ was raised from the dead, we shall be raised. It is simply and solely because Christ is glorified we shall be glorified. All comes from Him. There is not and never will be a sinner saved or exalted or glorified by or in any other than the Crucified Messiah of Israel. My dear friend, do you know Him of whom I speak? Have you any connection whatever with this Jesus of Nazareth? I ask it because I would have you to find in Him that which will make you happy both in this life and in the life to come. I ask you because He died for you and is ready and willing to save you. I ask you in order that you too may look forward not with fear but with joy to the glorious day of His coming. Think then of these things. Turn to Jesus. If you have been casting your net in on the side of the world and have caught nothing, take it up and cast it in on the other side. Oh, on this "other side" you will find everything—all you can need! With Jesus there is mercy and hope and joy. The world, nor death, nor hell can have more terrors. They all pass away in Christ. Moreover " when Christ, who is our life, shall appear, then shall ye also appear with Him in glory."

May God grant this may be the end of all who may read these pages: for the Lord Jesus Christ's sake. Amen.

SERMON VI.

THE LOVE OF GOD.

I St John iv. 19.—" We love Him, because He first loved us."

WE love Him—not all perhaps who may read this, for some I fear do not think enough of Him to love Him—but we, who are faithful to our calling. There is not, indeed, a true Christian living whose heart does not overflow with love for his God. The Lord's people are full of love. We see this love irradiating their lives and spurring them on to noble actions and great deeds. They are willing to follow Him whom they love wherever He may lead, whether it be into the paths of stormy trial or into the ways of pleasantness and peace. Whatever He sends to them, no matter if it be the cup of sorrow or the wine of joy, they accept it gladly because they love Him. The heavy cross, the dark night, the rough road, are as nothing when that deep love supports the burden. We can give our all, our own selves, our very lives, to the God for whom we have so much love.

And when we think of all this we are oftentimes led to ask ourselves the question: why should we thus love God? Why should men and women have such love that they are able to do anything, risk anything, lose everything for the sake of their Master?

And then our thoughts immediately run upon what He has done for us. We think of this beautiful world of ours with all its teeming wonders and glorious attractions. We remember how God has made everything subservient to our comforts and wants. The seasons come and go, day and night follow upon each other's steps, the ground gives of her increase, and we are fed and clothed and kept by a Father who cares for us, and not only for us but for the little homeless sparrow that flits from branch to branch, and housetop to housetop around us. This wonderful providence exercised over us is enough to make us love Him. But did it? The people of the world see and know these things as well as we, but do they actually make them love God? No, there must be something far beyond this that shall melt our hard hearts and fill them with divine love.

Then if the reason for our love be not in what God has done for our bodies, is it not to be found in what He has done for our souls? He gave His own Son for our salvation. That Son came down to earth and was tried, and suffered, and died, that we might live. The cruel taunt and the thorny crown, and the horrible cross were all endured for our sakes. The Lord Jesus had no need to die for Himself, but He loved us, and gave Himself for us.

Every drop of blood was shed, every pain undergone, every anguish suffered that we might enter into His glory. It was all done for us—for you, dear friend, and for me—that He might redeem us from death, and present us as His own before the Throne of His Father. Is not this enough to make men love Him? When we look upon the work of Christ can we help wondering that there should be a single soul left in our midst that is not burning with love? Yet we find it so. And though the thought of Christ's salvation indeed fills us with gratitude, yet we must go even deeper than that before we reach the mainspring of love.

We have the cause of it all given us in our text. "We love Him because He first loved us." What a startling truth! "Because He first loved us!" Before we ever loved Him He loved us!

When we were little children utterly ignorant of Him—when we were sitting in the great darkness and knew nothing of the God that made us or the God that saved us—He loved us. His bowels of compassion yearned for us that He might bring us unto Himself!

And so when we were unworthy of His love it was just the same. We were sinners against Him, despisers of His laws, rebels in His sight; there was not a single trait in us to recommend us to Him—our very righteousness was as filthy rags—our very obedience was sin—and yet He loved us! Yea, and

He could say unto us, "I have loved thee with an everlasting love!" Was there ever such love as this? When we love it is because we think we see something worthy of our love in the object of it; but God saw nothing in us—no beauty, no comeliness, naught but sin, and need, and unworthiness. Could we have loved like Him? And yet in all that ignorance and sin He loved us!

And here a thought comes upon us that at once leads us to a grand fundamental gospel truth. We hear men tell us that we must try and merit that love. And we see people everywhere acting upon that recommendation. They are indeed doing their very best to win God's favour. Everything that is told them to do, they do. They work, and work, and work. They may go on pilgrimages, or lacerate their bodies, or immure themselves in dark convents, in order to gain the prize that the teachers of the law of works hold out to them. What useless labour! What a waste of energy! The love they would obtain is already theirs! If they have in their hearts the least spark of love towards God, it is there not because they have earned it, or because they have merited it, but because God first loved them. We cannot get before God in this matter. The first love can never be on our side. It must be on God's. And it is given to us as love is always given, freely and without price. If God first loved us—loved us when we were in ignorance and sin—

He needs none of our miserable works to move Him. We cannot buy that love! Nothing we can offer could ever be an equivalent for such a priceless treasure. We are not worthy of it and we never can be. Then let us cast to the winds the false doctrine held before us of meriting it. No amount of tears and prayers and fastings and good works can give us what is already ours. We have now God's love. God loves every man, woman and child kneeling at His footstool. He is first and ever will be first in this question. Let us then accept His love as a free and royal sovereign gift. Let us yield to Him the right; yea crown Him Lord of all!

It is in this very fact—that when we were strangers and aliens, lost and ruined, sinful and unworthy—loving the things of this world rather than the things of the world to come— God loved us, that we love Him. That wonderful, unfathomable love of His is the secret of it all. That is the power that touches our cold, dead hearts and makes them live. That is the influence that compels us to weep the bitter tears of repentance over our sins, and to fall prostrate before the throne of Grace for forgiveness. We cannot remain forever alienated from the God who loves us so much, as to bear with us in our wickedness, and to spare us from the just punishment we have indeed deserved. We must love One who loved us so much that He gave His only begotten Son that through

His death we might receive eternal life. It is love begetting love.

We oftentimes meet with instances in ordinary life that in a measure illustrate this love of God. Some years ago a young man was on trial before a judge in England. He was the son of pious, simple-hearted parents. They had watched over him and prayed for him and advised him; but it seemed to do no good. He rejected their counsel, and went on from bad to worse. And now he was sentenced to transportation for seven years. And away he went across the sea, and then in a strange land he had time to think. And as the day of his release drew near he made up his mind like another prodigal son, and said, " I will arise and go to my father, and say unto him, Father, I have sinned against heaven and before thee, and am no more worthy to be called thy son." And home he went—broken-spirited and ashamed—but when he was folded in the arms first of his mother and then of his father, the love burned through and through, and melted the last remnants of the stony heart. It was a touching moment. And when he asked them if they could ever love him again, they told him amid flowing tears and joyful smiles that they had loved him through all—loved him when a criminal, loved him when a convict.

That was love touching upon the love of God, and yet as inferior to it as a little pool of water is inferior to the vast and boundless ocean. When we come to God we find ourselves no strangers there—it is, "My son, my son!" and "My Father, O my Father!" When we are brought to our senses and see the tremendous guilt of our sin—when we see that we are among the chief of sinners—and the home-longing comes into our heart, and we feel that we must go to our heavenly Father, we go on our way, it may be sad and doubtful, but when we get there and see how He loves us and learn how He has ever loved us, even the inestimable gift of the forgiveness of sin pales and fades before the wonderfulness and glory of that deep, everlasting love! The last shadow of doubt passes away, the last tinge of reserve vanishes, we yield ourselves up entirely without holding back—and we are His! O joy transcending joy—we love Him because then we find that He first loved us!

Is not this comfort for the sinner? Is not this good news for the returning penitent? The sins have indeed been many—who can tell the sum of them? for they are as numberless as the sands upon the seashore—and had they been punished as they indeed deserved we should not now be in a state of grace, within the reach of the exercise of mercy. But God loves us—loves the darkest and the deepest stained soul in our midst—and would save all from the curse we are bringing upon ourselves. There is not a sin added by us to our already vast multitude that does not wound the tender-hearted, loving Lord. We are grieving Him every day: we are despising the salvation He wrought for us at such a terrible cost: we are even putting Him to an open shame; and yet He says unto us, "Come unto me and I will give you rest:" "though your sins be as scarlet they shall be as white as snow, though they be red like crimson they shall be as wool." Can we refuse that call? Oh, my dear reader, if it be that you are among those who are far from God in the darkness of this world's sin, can you turn a deaf ear to this exhibition of divine love? Such glad tidings as this are enough to overpower the most obstinate soul. Just as we are—worthless, wretched, under sentence of death, without a spark of love towards Him—He loves enough not only to give us all He has, but to die for us. And oh if He loves us so much will He turn away from us when we go to Him and acknowledge our great wickedness? No, never! He cries, "Come unto Me, oh come unto Me!" Simply come—without preparation, without money, without righteousness—only come; and His love will do the rest. How passing strange that men and women would rather stay as strangers in this wilderness—hungry and thirsty, without a home—when they might live in a very heaven on earth, would they but accept this freely offered love of God! The comfort and the joy of loving God they had rather be without. What will be their remorse when they find hereafter that the day of grace is passed, and the arm of justice has forever stayed the overflowings of mercy! Then let us take to our hearts the deep truth of our text, and in the love of God turn to Him and live.

But our text has comfort for more than the sinner. It speaks to the widow, and the orphan, and the outcast. These are they who stand in need of great comfort. Sometimes it seems to them as though they were alone in the world—as though no one cared for them. But there is One who cares; there is One who loves. God is still theirs. He loves them. He shall make the widow's heart to sing for joy. He shall feed and provide for the fatherless. He shall gather in the outcast. No one can be alone who has God with him. And God is with us. His eye is ever upon us. Even the very hairs of our head are all numbered. There is not a sparrow falls to the ground without God's knowledge. And if he thus cares for such an insignificant thing as a sparrow shall He not much more care for us for whose souls the blood of the Lord Jesus was outpoured? Because we have bitter trials sent us that is no evidence that God does not love us. We are told that Jesus loved Martha, and her sister, and Lazarus, and yet He permitted death to enter that home and take the support and loved one of the family out of the sight of men. And if God has visited us with like afflictions, we may ever rely upon His love. It is still ours; and it can cheer our hearts when we find ourselves left alone and all our loved ones taken from us. Nothing can take away God's love. Neither the fires of martyrdom, nor the persecution of the enemies of the faith, nor even death itself can ever rob us of that. When all else is gone there is still a God whom we can call " our Father," and we know that His love is unchangeable and undying. There is an inexhaustible mine of comfort for us in that mighty truth.

And not only for those of us who are called upon to take that bitter part in life, but also for all whose path leads through any trial. It may be we are among the oppressed ones of the earth. Every man's hand seems against us. We are absolutely friendless. Or it may be we are numbered with the afflicted. Sickness and disease fill our days with sorrow and make us almost wish the last step in life's sad pilgrimage were taken. In either of these cases the consciousness of the love of God is indeed precious. Every pain we feel, every sigh that rends our heart, is known and felt by One who sympathizes with us and has made the sufferings of His people His own. Those sorrows make us fellow-sufferers with Him. And if that be true in reference to the things of this life, how much more is it true in reference to the things pertaining to the spirit! We all know how hard it is to keep in the narrow way of the Christian's walk. Temptations of all sorts come upon us and try to lead us astray. Sin is ever watching for an opportunity to overthrow us. But the terrible trial of the soul is when it is brought into the valley of the great shadow. There is no sun to cheer us in that cloud-benighted place. There seems to be no evidence that God is with us. We feel that He has forsaken us. He does not seem so near as in the old days when we were lying at the foot of the cross. And yet the love—the everlasting love—is indeed the same. The clouds of doubt may hide from our gaze the face of the blessed Saviour —the lying Adversary may tell us He is no longer ours—but no clouds, no Adversary, can touch the first love of our God. God is ever the same—the same yesterday, to-day and forever; we may change but He never! If He loved us in the bright days, He will love us in the dark as well. If He loved us when we were in the sunshine, He will never leave us nor forsake us, now we are under the cloud. We may well then rejoice and be glad! God's love encircles us on every side. Turn where we will there it meets us. In life and in death, in sorrow and in joy, in sin and affliction and tribulation—still ever and ever and ever the same. Oh, what a wonderful love! Oh, what a loving God! Wandering in the wilderness, pleading for mercy, outcast and forsaken, sick and dying, this love transcending all knowledge is caring for us, watching over us, saving us. It is ever flowing from God to man; it is surrounding us in our homes and in our lives like some mighty ocean, every ripple of which is the bearer of some unlooked-for mercy, every depth of which contains some rich and priceless treasure!

Such is the love of God—such is the love He has for every one. "He first loved us!" And what is our love for Him? What is our affection for Him who loved us and gave Himself for us? Do we love Him at all? That is the question of all questions for us to ask ourselves. There may be some who read this that have need to find an answer to it. There may be some whose hearts are very sad because they know nothing of this love. It is not God's fault; He loves them, and He would have them love Him. Oh, that every soul were touched, yea burning with this love! God asks us to yield Him our love. How can we refuse? How can we say Him nay, after all He has done for us? Shall these mercies vouchsafed us every day—shall these gracious invitations to come home—shall the sufferings and the death of the Son of God, all go for nought? Shame be to us if we have no gratitude in our souls for all those blessings! Shame be to us if we hold back from God that which is His due! If He has bought our souls from death let us yield them up to Him. If He loves us let us love Him. Let us give to Him our all!

And yet what is that all? Even when we love Him what is that love? Oh, how weak! Trembling and doubting and changing! Burning one day and cold the next! Utter'y without dependence! Compared with God's love it is as the feeble rushlight beside the overwhelming glory of the sun. Compared with God's love it is as the fading blade of grass beneath the mighty branches of the giant oak. It is nothing—and yet it is our all! And God wants that all. He asks for it now of you, my dear, though unknown, reader. "My son, give me thine heart." It may be worthless, it may be full of sin, it may be dead; but whatever it be, "My son, give me thine heart." And so the love may be very feeble and very flickering, yet that is the love God wants us to give Him, that is the love for which He is longing.

Beloved friend, would you be freed from sin, would you have this life lit up with a heavenly radiance, would you enter that glorious home which the Saviour has gone to prepare? God offers all this, and more than this, to every one. It may all be yours. There is not a single gift in our Father's hand that He would not have us share. He has done everything for us He could do because He loved us. He will do whatever we ask Him to do because He still loves us. And when we accept all these proffered blessings, when we make Him our Lord and our Master, when we learn to love Him, we shall love Him not because of the blessings or the gift or even the salvation, no, but we shall love Him because He first loved us. This is the grand lesson God would have us to learn. This is the wonderful truth that will fill us with adoring admiration all through the endless eternity. Why God should love such worthless, undeserving wretches as we are, we know not, and probably never shall know. But the fact remains the same, and that fact will enkindle our souls and make them still more fervent. When we ask one another in that better land why we love God, we shall answer as we answer now to-day—" We love Him because He first loved us."

May God give us of His grace that we may realize His love, and in return give to Him that which He asks of us, not as payment, not as the work of merit, but as the evidence of heartfelt gratitude ; for the Lord Jesus Christ's sake. Amen.

SERMON VII.

THE LOVE OF THE LORD JESUS.

St. John xiii. 1.—"Now before the feast of the passover, when Jesus knew that His hour was come that He should depart out of this world unto the Father, having loved His own which were in the world, He loved them unto the end."

OUR text takes us back to the night before the Crucifixion. Events the most solemn and heart-touching immediately recur to us. We cannot think of those events without perceiving in them an importance at once great and personal. The last words of Jesus given to His disciples in the upper chamber where they had celebrated the last Passover; the agony in the garden of Gethsemane; the institution of the Holy Communion; the betrayal and the trial of the Son of God before the Roman Governor and the Jewish High Priest, have an interest for us second only to the events of the following day and the glory of the Easter morn. We see in them the light of infinite love. We know that nought but love could have induced the Saviour of the world to give Himself up to a humiliation so great, to a death so severe. The grand secret of that noble life of sorrow and suffering was love, simply love for the souls of men. And never was that love displayed in more trying circumstances or in greater glory than on this solemn night. We may well think of such love as this. There is comfort for us in so doing, and strength for us in our weakness.

The text we have before us speaks particularly of the love of Jesus. It is a text full of suggestive thoughts. We shall get at them best if we look at some of the characteristics of this love. There are three features of it brought prominently before us.

In the *first* place it is an ENDURING LOVE. The text says that " When Jesus knew that His hour was come that He should depart out of this world unto the Father, having loved His own which were in the world, He loved them unto the end." Consider what is implied in the words " Jesus knew that His hour was come." There is an appointed time unto all men when to die, but God in His mercy has withheld the knowledge of it from us. We have no idea when the day of our death will come. How unhappy we should be if we did know! We should look forward to the day with dread! Our lives would be embittered with the thought that at a given moment all would end. Yet this knowledge was added to Christ's sorrow. He knew the day of His death. He knew the hour when " He should depart out of this world unto the Father." The agony of death stared Him in the face. The purple robe, the crown of thorns, the cross, the grave, were all before Him. Each moment was bearing Him on the stream of time nearer and nearer to that awful hour. His soul was bowed down with anguish and grief. His hand was already on the cup of gall and His lips had tasted its bitterness. He saw that terrible future close at hand. And yet knowing and feeling all this His love was as true as ever for His disciples. Where our affection would have grown less, His became stronger. "Having loved His own which were in the world," in the time past, He loves them now,—"He loves them unto the end." What a blessed thought this is! Nought can destroy the love of Christ for His people. Neither time, nor sorrow, nor death can change Him. He is "the same yesterday, to-day, and forever." He loves unto the end!

Among the many good things which God has given us in this life, the assurance of such lasting, enduring love is the greatest of all. Before we had any love for Him, nay, before we were capable of loving Him, our Lord Jesus loved us and gave Himself for us. Back in the ages of eternity our names were written upon His heart. Ere the foundations of the earth were laid we were precious in His sight. "We love Him because He first loved us." And all down the ages His love has still remained. He loved us when seated on the Throne of His power. He loved us when a wanderer and a sufferer here among men. He loved us when His soul was in the bitterness of despair. He loved us when hanging on the cross. He loves us now that He has ascended to the right hand of the Majesty on high. And He will love us still when He comes in clouds to judge the world. He loves unto the end. No change in His circumstances has ever or will ever change His nature. Whether He be as the Eternal God or the lowly man, the dying Saviour or the exalted Redeemer, the successful Intercessor or the all-powerful Judge, His love is ever the same. Having once loved, He loves for ever.

This can be said of no one else. We are constantly changing. Circumstances affect us. Absence effaces many a fond love. An idle story will weaken a strong affection. A misunderstanding will quench a burning fondness. But nothing touches the love of Christ. That is more constant than the sun in his strength, or the great rock in its stability, or the revolving worlds in their obedience to the laws of the universe. "I have loved thee," says God to Israel, "with an everlasting love." "I am the Lord, I change not." And so St. Paul exclaims in an outburst of glad rapture, "I am persuaded that neither death, nor life, nor angels, nor principalities, nor powers, nor things present, nor things to come, nor height, nor depth, nor any other creature, shall be able to separate us from the love of God which is in Christ Jesus our Lord." We may change, but He never. Our love may grow cold, but His love will ever burn. The chill of approaching death may weaken our memory of earthly friends, but no death will endanger His memory or weaken His love. He has ever and will ever love the same. Blessed truth! "Having loved His own which were in the world, He loved them unto the end." What a privilege is ours to be the objects of such eternal love! How we should rejoice and be glad at the thought of it! What an effect it ought to have on our lives! May we realize this now! May we know that we are indeed among God's own people! May we hear Him say, amid the disappointments of this world:—

> "Mine is an unchanging love,
> Higher than the heights above,
> Deeper than the depths beneath,
> Free and faithful, strong as death."

It is an enduring love. This is one feature of it suggested by our text.

But in the *second* place it is a PATIENT LOVE. When Jesus was with His disciples in that upper room, He knew that that very night one of their number would betray Him into the hands of His enemies; another, now the loudest in his professions, would deny that he ever knew Him, and all of them together would forsake Him and flee. And yet He loved them unto the end. There was poor Peter and unbelieving Thomas and the spiritually-minded John —all afraid to go with Him, still He loved them. What a glorious feature is this of Christ's love! Even we with our many shortcomings, cannot touch that love! It is a very Eddystone light that all the fury of a raging ocean cannot put out. It is as the bright sun; no cloud, no storm can rob it of its glory. Sooner shall the mighty ocean be dried up and this world scattered into atoms, and the vast universe itself fall to dust and pass away, than that the patient love of Christ shall be withdrawn from His people. They may fall, they may sin, they may even deny the faith—yet His love is still with them, overshadowing them, protecting them, leading them. Sin may cast them down, yet the arm of His power shall raise them up. Sorrow may encloud their lives, yet the rays of His glory shall light up the gloom. The sharp-pointed arrows of persecution and fear and tribulation may sink deep into their hearts, but the rankling wounds shall be healed with the balm of His patient, constant, consoling love. There is great joy in all this. If the love of Christ were only ours when we deserved it we should never possess it or experience it. Our poor, weak nature could never earn, and never retain love so rich, so precious, so patient as that of the Saviour's. God knows this, and therefore He gives His love and all His gifts freely without money and without price. He bears with our infirmities. He has compassion upon our weakness. Yea, though He knows that we shall speedily fall into sin, yet He loves us. His love is most constant. He loves us in all our sin.

This has been the experience of God's people in all ages of the world. Though Adam and Eve disobeyed God in Eden, yet His love provided a

Mediator who should reconcile erring humanity and offended Deity. Lot erred by living in sinful Sodom, but God's love brought him out. David sinned most grievously, yet he was surrounded with sure mercies. Elijah hid himself in the wilderness, and though God punished him by appointing his successor, yet the old prophet was carried to heaven by horses and chariot of fire. And so with the apostles. Thomas and Peter, and all that forsook their Lord and fled were not left by their God. What would have been the end of those men of old had God's love not been patient and constant? What would become of us were our sins taken into account by a just God? Not one would attain the promises. Not one would enter into glory. It is because God's love is constant that we are saved. It is because He is patient with us that we have a good hope of the future. While we were yet sinners Christ died for us. There was nothing to recommend man to God, and yet " God so loved the world that He gave His only begotten Son that whosoever believeth in Him should not perish but have everlasting life." And so great was the love of Christ that He accepted every indignity for man's sake. The cruel taunt, the unbelief, the persecution that greeted Him here below did not deter Him from His purpose. His love was immutable, constant, eternal, patient. Though He knew the weakness of the disciples He loved them unto the end. And so with us His love changeth not. "For a small moment have I forsaken thee; but with great mercies will I gather thee. In a little wrath I hid my face from thee for a moment; but with everlasting kindness will I have mercy on thee, saith the Lord thy Redeemer. For this is as the waters of Noah unto me: for as I have sworn that the waters of Noah should no more go over the earth; so have I sworn that I would not be wroth with thee, nor rebuke thee. For the mountains shall depart, and the hills be removed; but my kindness shall not depart from thee, neither shall the covenant of my peace be removed, saith the Lord that hath mercy on thee."

There is great comfort in these words. Christ does not get weary of His people. He loves them to the last. It is a love that passeth knowledge. It is one of those things that even the angels of God "desire to look into." That Christ should never be tired of the endless backslidings of His people, but always ready to forgive and forget their shortcomings tells of a love that the heart of man can never grasp. It is a grand truth. Those whom Jesus receives He always keeps. Those whom He loves at first He loves at last. His promise shall never be broken: "Him that cometh unto Me I will in no wise cast out." "Having loved His own which were in the world," in spite of their failings, "He loved them unto the end." His love is a patient love.

In the *third* place it is a PERSONAL LOVE.

Its greatest comfort consists in this. The religion of the Lord Jesus is entirely a personal religion. He was personal in His life here on earth. "He calleth His own sheep by name. To every one of His flock He says, "I have called thee by thy name, thou art mine." To one of those who had sat with Him around that passover table He had said, "Simon, Simon, behold Satan hath desired to have you, that he may sift you as wheat, but I have prayed for thee that thy faith fail not." And when we are going astray, like lost sheep, the Chief Shepherd does not forget us. "He restoreth my soul." He looks after the wandering one, and when he has found it, He lifts it to His shoulder rejoicing; or if it be a lamb He carries it in His bosom back to the fold, not as a member of the general flock, but as His own dear Mary or Martha or James or John, whose Christian name was so recorded in the book of life before the world began. This special, personal love is characteristic of Christ. Though in a sense He loved the world, yet it was His own which were in the world that He loved unto the end. This would imply that He has a special people—that there are those among men that He can specially call His own. And such, Scripture teaches us, is the case. Again and again God declares that there are those whom He will call His people and who shall call Him their God. Those whom He has called to a knowledge of the Truth, justified by the blood of the Cross and sanctified by

His Holy Spirit—these are the people of God. And those, whether near or afar off, who are trying to follow in the footsteps of the Master, who are seeking to do His will and to partake of His love—these are precious in His sight. For them He died. For them He has entered the Holy of Holies. For them He stands ever interceding in the presence of the Father. He loves each one of them. He loves them individually. Not a trouble or a sorrow that they have is unnoticed by Him. The very hairs of their head are all numbered. He prays for them, leads them, blesses them. They owe everything to his love. "I live," says St. Paul, "by the faith of the Son of God, who loved me and gave Himself for me."

The test of His love is in the fact of His death. Had He not great love He never could have died for us. He looked upon the small company assembled around Him and though He knew the agony that was already seizing His soul and the death that awaited Him on the morrow, yet it was all for those loved ones and for the other sheep far adown the ages, and it was enough. They were poor, weak, wandering ones—all their right to heaven had been forfeited—they were rebels against God, but He loved them, and that love sustained Him in the gloom of death. And so He says to each one of us, "I will never leave thee nor forsake thee." "Having loved His own which were in the world He loved them unto the end." And, oh, what love! Who knows its boundless depths, its borderless expanse?

> "Oh, this no tongue can utter; this
> No mortal page can show;
> The love of Jesus, what it is,
> None but His loved ones know."

Yet this love is for you and me, my reader, not as a nation, or a society, or a congregation, but as individuals. He loves each one of His people as though there were none but that one in the world. He suffered and died and rose again for us as individuals. We are regenerated and justified and sanctified as individuals. And so we shall be saved and spend eternity in heaven. We were in the Saviour's mind in all His sorrowing and suffering. We are thus in His mind now He is exalted a Prince in His Father's house. And thus we shall ever be. He will always have a special love for each one of His followers. His love is a personal love.

We may well rejoice that the love of our Saviour Christ's, is such as this. There is comfort in the fact that it is *enduring*—nothing in Him can ever change it; that it is *patient*—nothing in us can ever change the love in him; that it is *personal*—for each one individually. Such love as this can sustain us in all trials—in life and in death. It can heal the sorrows of the afflicted and satisfy the longings of the awakened heart. Such love can be found nowhere else than in Christ. No one loves us and cares for us as He does. We have no greater friend. He loved us enough to die for us. " Greater love hath no man than this that a man lay down his life for his friends." Well then may we exclaim with the Apostle: " Unto Him that loved us, and washed us from our sins in His own blood, and hath made us kings and priests unto God and His Father to Him be glory and dominion for ever and ever."

Christian reader, Christ would have you remember that love of His. He would have you keep it ever in mind. Let your heart then be filled with love like His. Consecrate yourself anew to Him. Strive to serve Him better in the time to come than you have ever done in the time past. We have strong assurances of His love. We know that He loves us though He were in the hand of death, yea, though we were about to desert Him and to deny that we ever knew Him. Have we no love to return ? Have we no empty hearts to give Him to be filled with His love ? Have we no spare moments to devote to His service ? No talents—nothing to use for Him ? Think of what He did for us and then can we not say—

> " Were the whole realm of nature mine,
> That were an offering far too small ;
> Love so amazing—so divine—
> Demands my soul, my life, my all."

Let us give Him then our soul, our life, our all.

And may this very hour be the beginning of a renewed life in which we shall shew forth our gratitude for all He has done for us; in which we shall grow more and more like unto Him, more and more meet for the Redeemer's kingdom.

SERMON VIII.

SALVATION THE EFFECT OF MERCY.

ROMANS IX. 16.—" So then it is not of him that willeth, nor of him that runneth, but of God that sheweth mercy."

AS soon as we behold the reality and awfulness of sin, and become vividly aware of the dangers to which it exposes us, and the terrible end to which it is hastening us, the question that comes to us again and again till it be answered is "What must I do to be saved? How shall I escape the certain wrath that awaits the workers of iniquity?" And though this question is a perfectly proper one, and one that I wish to God every soul on the face of the earth would put to itself, yet when we first ask it we almost invariably throw all our stress upon the personality of it: what must *I do?* And we do this in such a manner as by our emphasis almost to change the question into "What work must I do in order to save myself?"

The question in this form is perfectly natural. It is thoroughly in harmony with the views and opinions of the natural man. Were we to reason about it we should conclude that not only was something absolutely necessary to be done but that it must be done by *us*. And as a matter of fact we find multitudes of honest-minded and sin-conscious people labouring hard to make for themselves some way of deliverance from the power and consequences of sin. Some are working one way and some another. We see many launch out into a rigid observance of the law of ceremonies : others into as strict an obedience to the principles of morality. They place themselves in bondage to one or other of those departments of the system of works. They hope by this outward discipline to attain the desired end. They thus think they are working out their own salvation.

And if salvation depended upon merit and could be earned by our good works, taking into consideration the infirmities of the flesh, they certainly deserve the reward for which they are striving. There is a man who fasts often and spends hours in prayer. Nothing keeps him from the house of God and he is always in his place at the Holy Communion. To do this costs him much sacrifice, but that he makes willingly as indeed he should, and though there is no harm but much good to be derived from his observances, yet ask him what his hope of salvation is, and if he be true to the thought of his heart he will tell us he is resting it upon this ritual rule. " I have been," he will say, "a regular attendant at Church and at the means of grace all my days, and thus having done my best to serve God, I know He will not forget me."

Or take the moral man. He never wronged anyone in his life ; rather than injure another he has sacrificed himself. A lie or an oath never crosses his lips nor is he in any sense intemperate in any of his habits. His rule has been to do to others as he would have them do to him, and all this is very proper and very necessary, but he builds up his hope upon this strict and honest life. And whether a man follows out either of these rules of conduct, or both, depend upon it, if he looks upon what he is doing as conducive to salvation, he will throw all his powers into the task. And as he learns more of the law of God he will strive to keep the whole law, and thus do his best to run after eternal life and freedom from sin.

I have no fault to find just here with either the law of ceremonies, or the law of morality : both are right enough in their way ; but it is with the false hope attached to them I have to deal. That hope is at once the most popular, and the most delusive of all hopes. There is hardly an individual that does not endanger himself with it at the very first step he takes after the conviction of sin. "I will do this and I will do that, and all will be well." And it makes no difference how many whitened bones lie on that shore of wrecks, the victims of the law of works, there are plenty more ready to die there.

Surely a very little thought would convince us of the impossibility of earning salvation ourselves. Suppose we undertake to keep the whole law : wh can tell how oft he offendeth ? That law must not be violated one iota in thought, word, or deed. And yet who is there that is not all the time sinning in thought? We think sin though we do not express it, and that very thinking, our Saviour teaches us is sin· Experience must have proved to us again and again' that we cannot keep straight in the narrow path of God's righteous law. We are going astray all the days of our life. Do what we will we cannot always resist the voice of temptation. Were we to succeed in avoiding certain given sins we should plunge ourselves into some other sin. We should be proud that we were righteous, and thus be guilty of the foundation sin of all. As long as we are men and women here in the flesh we shall never be perfect, never be able to keep from iniquity.

If this is the fact, and who can deny it? how foolish is it for the awakened sinner to think of doing that which is impossible! Why emphasize "What must I do?" when he can do nothing? Why put his trust in ceremonies and morality when he can really keep the law of neither? The truth is that whatever he does before justification is sin. He is working for justification, but until he is justified all his good works go for nothing. This is a startling fact. It may be hard to believe. But it is the doctrine of the Church of England. The thirteenth Article says of works done before justification "we doubt not but they have the nature of sin." It is the doctrine of the Word of God. There we are told that "the sacrifice of the wicked is an abomination to the Lord." It may be outwardly the same as the justified man's, but still it is an abomination, it is sin. The case of the man then who would make himself just with God—and to be justified is equivalent to being saved—is indeed a desperate one. Instead of escaping from sin he still remains in sin, and binds himself more and more in its iron fetters. He is in a hopeless bondage.

Our text brings before us this great truth. When we ask "What must I do to be saved?" we must remember that "It is not of him that willeth, nor of him that runneth, but of God that sheweth mercy." We may want salvation, and we may run after salvation, but salvation is obtained neither by wishing, nor running, but of the free, sovereign grace of God. It is given by Him without money and without price. No observances, no laws, no works can ever gain for us that inestimable gift. We may do and do all the days of our life, but we will never save ourselves. Salvation comes not from doing, but from God. That is an important fact.

And it is as reasonable as it is important. The Scriptures teach us that God sent His Son into the world to save man. He lived here below and died on the Cross that He might save us from eternal death. Now if salvation comes from us, from what we do, then it does not come from the Lord Jesus Christ, and if so, all His work was useless. If He is not the One who saves, but we are our own saviours, then His sufferings and cruel death were altogether unnecessary, and actually thrown away. It was because God saw that we were helpless, it was because He saw we were so entangled in sin, and so could not deliver ourselves from the doom to which that sin was hurrying us, that He sent to us a Redeemer, One mighty to save. He knew our utter inability better than we could ever know it, and pity for us in our desperate condition made Him extend to us a salvation. And the simple question then is: Was the work of Christ complete and perfect, or was it defective and partial? Did Christ really succeed in saving man, or is man in the same condition he was in immediately after the fall?

There can be but one answer to the question when put in this way. It is an impossibility for God to fail in anything. When He created the heavens and the earth, and reviewed His marvellous work, He pronounced that it was very good; and when He hung upon the Cross, and looked upon the salvation of the human race, He declared to all the world "It is finished." And when those words dropped from the lips of the Divine Incarnation they were very truth. The work of salvation actually was finished, and finished as God finishes everything, perfect and entire. It could not be otherwise. To say that God sent His Son into the world to save the world, and that His purpose was not accomplished, is to say that He is not Almighty, and that His wisdom was at fault. We cannot conceive such a thing as that. We cannot for an instant conceive that Christ came short in any sense of fulfilling His work, of verily and completely saving man from sin and the wrath to come.

Thus we see that salvation is not of man, but of God. "So that it is not of him that willeth, nor of him that runneth, but of God that sheweth mercy." And when the awakened sinner learns this truth he will learn to cease to look upon what he must do, and will forget himself in gazing upon what Christ has done. He will no longer rest his hopes upon a ceremonial or a moral life, or even upon a godly one, but upon the Crucified Messiah of Israel. It will no longer be "See what I am doing," but "Behold the Lamb of God that taketh away the sin of the world." There is no more running after salvation, for he now knows that salvation is already his, that it is God's gracious gift to man.

Need I speak of the joy and strength and security this doctrine ensures to us? Is it not plain upon the very face of our text, that we have every hope? What hope does the law give us? We cannot keep it. If we break but one point the Scripture says we are guilty of all. And we are guilty, we are under its sentence, and that sentence is death. But if God saves us, nay, if He has saved us, we have then nothing to fear. We may rejoice and be glad when we know that the Lord Jesus Christ, by His death upon the Cross, made there a full, perfect and sufficient sacrifice, oblation and satisfaction for the sins of the whole world, and that in that finished work we are indeed saved.

There is, however, one duty that remains to us in reference to this question. Salvation is indeed of God, absolutely of God. It is a gift from Him to man: but it must be received. If we would avail ourselves of that salvation, it must be appropriated to us and by us. Otherwise we remain under sin and death by our own choice and act. And the means of appropriation, the way in which it is received, is Faith. It is not works, but simply believing. "Believe on the Lord Jesus Christ and thou shalt be saved." This is the doctrine that the Word of God enforces upon our attention again and again. Christ has died for us; Christ has saved us; and all God asks of us in order to salvation is that we accept it by faith. No gift is of use to the person for whom it is intended unless it be accepted. If a man be drowning in the mid ocean and a vessel comes near to the rescue and offers to save the man, and the man refuses the offer he must drown. If a captive in a strange land refuses to accept the ransom procured for him by his friends he must remain in his bondage. And so if we allow the work of God to go unaccepted what can God do more? He has done everything that could possibly be done, and there is not a man, woman or child, however full of sin they may have been, that may not be saved from that sin, and from eternal woe, if they will but receive the salvation.

And just here let us remember that when we say this salvation is ours, we also know that it is the only salvation which God has provided for us. There is no other that will avail us anything. There was no possibility of our entering into life eternal without the death of Christ. God gave Him, when every other way was closed up, and now there is no salvation in any other, "For there is none other name under heaven given among men whereby we must be saved." If then we refuse this salvation we can have no hope that God will save in any other way. It is through Christ and only through Christ we may enter heaven, and if we have not Christ then we can never have heaven. We may have a great deal but without this "one thing needful" we shall be lost. Nor has God any mercy for man save that which flows through His Son. All the love of the Infinite centres in him, and to those out of Christ there can be no love and no mercy. How foolish then for people to forget Christ, and yet trust all will be well! God will not save, God cannot save, except through the sacrifice of the Lord Jesus, and to those who reject Him there remaineth no more sacrifice for sins,, "but a certain fearful looking for of judgment and fiery indignation, which shall devour the adversaries."

Such being the case we see that salvation is not of him that willeth—we may will a thousand ways to glory and devise as many more, but that will help us nothing: nor is salvation of him that runneth—he may work all the days of his life but it is labour in vain; salvation comes only of God that sheweth mercy. So then the answer for the one who asks "What must I do to be saved?" is, Look to God for salvation—away from self, away from all, to the Lord Jesus—believe in Him and thou shalt be saved. That is all, no willing, no running, but altogether of God.

And for whom is this salvation wrought? To whom is it offered? Our text says it is of God that sheweth mercy. It is then a question of mercy: and where mercy is shown it is implied that it is shown to those who need it. All therefore who need mercy are the ones to whom the mercy is offered. It is then, my dear reader, offered to you and to me, for surely we need mercy: it is offered to all who feel that they are helpless and undone. Perhaps some one is reading this who is in just that condition. It very often happens that many who begin to think about these things hesitate to come to God because they feel themselves so utterly unworthy. They stay away trusting to make themselves better before they come. The fact is they want to justify and save themselves first and come to God afterwards. They are very much like a sick man who says to himself that when he gets better he will go to the physician. If it is absurd in the one case, it is equally as absurd in the other. And as a matter of fact the man who waits to fit himself for God is just as unfit after a long endeavour as he was at the beginning. And if God's grace be working in him he soon finds himself in a desperate case. He can do nothing, and he realizes the awful blackness of his soul. That man is just the one in need of mercy and until he has received mercy—until he has received the heavenly medicine—he will be no better. Why not then acknowledge that he is in the terrible plight? It is mercy he needs and that is just what God offers him. It is not when he is well he needs a physician—it is not when he is saved he needs a Saviour—but it is when he is dying, dying in sin, that he requires strength and assistance. And it is then God offers him salvation. "I came not to call the righteous but sinners to repentance." And so he calls unto Him, not the hale, the hearty, and the strong, but the weary and the heavy-laden, that He may give them rest. It is just these poor, helpless, worn-out sinners, who need salvation for whom salvation was wrought. It is just those who can do nothing for whom God has done everything. It is to those who are floundering in the miry pit, and find it impossible to get out, God is extending a helping hand, and offering to set their feet upon the rock, yea, even upon the Rock of Ages!

Dear reader, are you among those to whom these words of the old, old story have a welcome application? I do not ask you if you are conscious of sin: I trust that is a point already admitted: but I ask the question which is of still more importance, Are you freed from the consequences of sin? Are you saved from the curse of the law? I am sure there are many who fain would be. I am sure there are many who are longing for reconciliation with God. But they feel they are still in the great bondage. It is to such I address myself. To whom are they looking for salvation? Is it to their own self, or to God? Is it to their own condition or works, or is it to the crucified Lord and Saviour? Suppose the leper that was in the great multitude which followed Jesus when He came down from the Mount on which He had just preached one of His wonderful sermons, had looked to himself, or had even mourned over his sad condition, would it have helped him any? Not in the least. But he looked to Jesus and he said "Lord, if thou wilt, thou canst make me clean." There was his hope, there was his life, and the cure which he never could have wrought himself was immediately wrought for him by the God of all power. So it is exactly with us who are afflicted with the leprosy of sin. We may look at our sin-spots as long as we like. We may weep over them. We may try to cover them up. The will may be very good, and the attempt may be very good. But that will not heal them. The disease will remain as bad as ever after all our work. Health and life and salvation must be of God. We must come to Him with our plague-smitten souls, and in the words of faith say unto Him "Lord, if thou wilt, thou canst make me clean." Are you thus, my dear reader, looking to the Lord? Are you convinced that "It is not of him that willeth, nor of him that runneth, but of God that sheweth mercy?" Then let us learn one other truth—the one to which the connection of my text more especially points—that not only is the salvation which we would have of God, but the very desire we have to obtain that salvation is of God. It is God who has taught us what sin is, it is God who has given us the fear of the evil to come it is God who has given us the will to escape both the sin and the evil. We have that consciousness, that fear, that will, not of ourselves, it is not inherent in us, but of God. Then let us give Him all the glory! Let us acknowledge that we are nothing and He is everything! Let us go before Him and forgetting self, forgetting our own paltry righteousness, plead for mercy, for nothing but mercy! That is what we want, that is what we must have.

Then when we lie at the foot of the cross we shall find that there is no "do" in the matter, but that it is all done. We shall not look forward to a future salvation, but to one already accomplished. And we shall rise rejoicing in the Lord, and then we shall work. Then we shall tell others what a dear Saviour we have found, we shall seek to add glory to His name and to His cause, and above all we shall endeavour by His grace to avoid the sin that so long enslaved us, the sin that so nearly wrought our ruin!

May God bless this message to the heart of every one who reads it, for the Lord Jesus Christ's sake. Amen.

SERMON IX.

THE VESSELS OF MERCY.

Romans ix. 23.—"That He might make known the riches of His glory on the vessels of mercy which He had afore prepared unto glory."

SUCH is the gracious purpose of God towards His people. They shall receive of the riches of His glory. They are specially prepared for this. It is part of the eternal plan on which God has worked from the very beginning. He Himself leads the sinner to the Cross. He finds him in the wilderness and He carries him to the fold, nor does He give him up until he is safe within the shelter. There is a comfort in this that no words can express. If we look into our text we shall find this is the lesson taught us there. God is with us from the first to the last. He is the Lord over all the way from sin unto glory, from death unto life. Such a view of salvation must compel us to sink man out of sight and to exalt and magnify the mercy and power and glory of God.

The very expression by which the apostle denominates God's people strengthens this doctrine—they are "vessels of mercy." A vessel is an utensil purposely made for holding. The one who makes it shapes and forms it as he pleases. The vessel has no voice in the matter at all. The potter has absolute power over the clay. So God says to the House of Israel "Cannot I do with you as this potter? Behold as the clay is in the potter's hand, so are ye in mine hand." The potter then has "power over the clay, of the same lump to make one vessel unto honour and another unto dishonour." And the Lord has a like power over us who are but as clay to mould us and to prepare us for whatever may be His purpose.

This fact teaches us our utter helplessness and absolute dependence on God. It destroys the idea that we control our own eternal destiny or save our own souls. We are simply in the hands of God. If we have a will to be saved it is because He has planted that will in our hearts. If we behold the glories of Redeeming Love it is because He has revealed them to us. If we overcome sin and temptation it is in His strength. If we reach heaven at last it is by His grace. We owe everything to Him. The first spark of spiritual life, the sense of forgiveness, the joys of the pilgrimage, the glory of the eternal day —all to Him. He has made us vessels—vessels for what? Why, to hold His mercy! That was His design. We were rebels against Him, sinners in His sight, but He would show us His mercy. We were but empty vessels but now are we full. Yes, and we are now full because we were once empty! Self was emptied out, and sin and guilt and the terrors of the law and the last dregs of self-righteousness—all and everything belonging to man, all emptied out and mercy poured in. And now we stand before God vessels of mercy—our title to come into His presence resting simply upon His mercy. Our only plea—His mercy; our only hope, our life, our joy—His mercy. Let this solemn fact never be forgotten. It is not what we are or what we have done but what God is and what He has done for us. It is not whether we are good or bad, but whether we are vessels of mercy. Have we been under the potter's hand? Have we been filled with the outflowings of Divine Love? If so, we are the ones of whom our text speaks. We are vessels of mercy prepared to receive of the riches of God's glory. Let us give the praise to God! Let our doubting hearts ascribe all the glory to His blessed name! He has done it all!

Consider another point. The text speaks of preparation: "which He had afore prepared unto glory." It needed preparation. We needed preparation in order to be filled with mercy and we needed still more preparation for glory. The materials all needed to be made ready for Solomon's magnificent Temple, and so we must be made ready for that still more glorious Temple not made with hands, eternal in the heavens. Sin must be conquered, evil passions must be subdued, a soul of iniquity must be regenerated and sanctified. Our affections, our love, our will, our life must all be changed. We must be moulded and cut and trimmed for Paradise. And how can all this be brought about? How can man be made meet for the Master's kingdom? Does not experience tell us, that we are powerless to accomplish this great result? "Who can bring a clean thing out of an unclean?" asks Job, and he answers, "not one!" No man can prepare himself for heaven. No man can free himself from sin. The trees of the forest cannot change their nature, neither can man change his. No man can turn at his own will from the paths of vice into the way of holiness. "Can the Ethiopian change his skin, or the leopard his spots?" If so, "then," adds Jeremiah, "may ye also do good, that are accustomed to do evil." And yet man must be changed. He must be born again. He must be prepared for the future. And there again our text throws the whole work upon God: "which He had afore prepared unto glory." He Himself, the Lord God Almighty, prepares His people for glory. He is the workman, we are the clay. He and He only who is Nature's Lord can change us from sinners into saints. He who conquered death can conquer sin. What a blessed thought this is! We are in His hands. He can touch our blinded sight and reveal to us the day of salvation. He can speak to the chaos of desolation that reigns in our hearts and "the desert shall rejoice and blossom as the rose." He can lead us from the City of Destruction to the City of Peace where dwell His ransomed ones in the mansions of eternal bliss.

See how mercy is connected with this preparation. "Vessels of mercy which He had afore prepared unto glory." And what is mercy but an act of love? Have we not suggested here the mode of God's preparation? Is it not by love? Are we not won to the Cross by the love and mercy we there see displayed? The hammer of affliction may scatter the fragments of stone but the fire of love alone can melt them. The thunders of Sinai may strike terror to the soul but the still small voice of mercy alone can quiet the raging tempest and still our doubts and fears. It is the "love of Christ that constraineth us." Nothing can hold and bind the sinner to the Saviour so strongly as the silken cords of Divine love cast around the trembling soul. Nothing can encourage us in the way or compel us to persevere unto the end more than the thought of the love God has for us. We cannot burst those bands of love, we cannot refuse to listen to that voice of mercy. We cannot help loving God for "God is love" and "we love Him because He first loved us."

But if we are won by love, are we not kept by love? Vessels of mercy—vessels filled with love! Remember how often we stumble and fall; how often temptation overcomes us and leads us into sin; how often we wander away. Yet God's love and mercy follows us, preserves us and lifts us up. Affliction is sent us, but it is from God. The dark, lowering clouds of adversity are tinged with the glory of the eternal love. The deep sea of tribulation is quiet and beautiful beneath the sunlight of mercy that rests upon its wavelets of sorrow. We drink of the bitter cup, but the hand that holds it to our lips trembles with love. It is all love; all the way through. Our sins are forgiven in love. Our heart's proudest idol is taken from us in love. Our stubborn wills are bent and broken in love. The whole preparation is a preparation of love. We know that God has done it all. He has prepared us Himself. He made us as vessels unto honour, and he has filled us with mercy. Our text tells us all this. We are nothing —nothing but "vessels of mercy which he had afore prepared unto glory"—nothing but the objects of redeeming love. Love found us, love ransomed us, love saved us. All round us nothing but love. Love within and love without. Love in this life, and everlasting love beyond the grave. Oh, what glory we should ascribe unto God for all this! How gladly we should laud and magnify His holy name! What was there in us that led Him to give His Son to die for our salvation? Nothing, nothing. It was His love that did it all. "God so loved the world that He gave His only begotten Son, that whosoever believeth in Him should not perish, but have everlasting life." Had it not been for God's love there had been no heaven for us! Had it not been for His mercy we should have remained in our sins justly condemned, the worthy objects of His righteous indignation. Oh, that we might realize this more and more! Oh, that we might feel ourselves to be nothing and hold Him to be All and in all, the Author and Finisher of our faith, the Lord God Almighty, just and true, the King of all His saints! Simply to lie at His feet—empty vessels to be filled with His mercy, to be prepared by Him for glory. That is our position. That is where our text suggests we ought to be.

But this is not all our text assures us of. It tells us of God's purpose concerning these vessels of mercy. He has not merely filled them with mercy or prepared them for glory, but it is his avowed intention to make known to them the riches of His glory. Elsewhere the Apostle speaks of the "riches of His goodness," and the "riches of His grace," both expressions referring to the same thing as the one before us. For when we see His goodness there we behold His grace, and when we behold His grace we are surrounded with the manifestation of His glory. God's goodness, grace and glory are all to be revealed and made known to the vessels of His mercy. And that, to a certain extent, in this life. "I had fainted," says David, " unless I had believed to see the goodness of the Lord in the land of the living." We shall see much of God's glory here. We shall behold His grace in His dealings with His people. The hand that has rescued us from danger and shielded us from the assaults of our enemies, and led us in the way, we shall recognize to be the hand of God. The blood stains that hide the sin-marks on our soul, the robe of righteousness that is cast over our guilt and shame, the voice that bids us stand before the throne of God, we shall assuredly find proceed from His love. Revelations will be made to us. The night of our pilgrimage will be cheered with the dawning of the eternal morn. We shall see God's glory resting upon the gloomy mountains of doubt that hem our narrow way. We shall behold His goodness wherever we are and in whatever we are doing. We shall feel the influences of His grace in our hearts. But what will all this be to the hereafter? Truly what we see and know now is as nothing to that which shall be revealed in the other world. After all we can know but little of God in this life. The veil hides the Holy of Holies from our view. A river rolls between us and Paradise. But the veil will be torn in sunder, the river will be passed, and we shall see Him as He is.

> "While here, alas, I know but half His love,
> But half discern Him, and but half adore;
> But when I meet Him in the realms above
> I hope to love Him better, praise Him more,
> And feel and tell amid the choir divine,
> How fully I am His, and He is mine."

What a positive assurance our text gives us that this will be our end! It is God's purpose to take us to Himself. It is His purpose to reveal to us the riches of His glory. Here again we see it is all cast upon God. It is God that will make known to us all things. We have nothing to do with it. It is a part of God's eternal plan. He makes, He prepares, He receives. He commences and He finishes the work. He fills us with mercy and He crowns us with glory. When the dark rain-clouds hang across the brightness of the sun we cannot remove them, nor can we touch the darker clouds that roll between us and God. We cannot remove the ocean-floods of sin and guilt that separate us from the land of peace. No, but God can. God can take away the floods and the clouds, and make the light of His countenance to shine upon us. And this He intends to do. He has prepared us for this, and He will assuredly bring us to it. We shall see the fulness of His glory.

How many are the thoughts suggested to us just here! What room is there for doubt? The promise rests upon God. He cannot lie. His word is sure. And not only this, but the work is His. He will bring it to pass. It cannot fail. We must receive the glory. No one can hinder us. No man can prevent the sun from shining upon the earth, neither can man prevent God's glory from shining upon His saints. Death shall remove the last obstacle. We know that the moon's light is but the reflection of the light of the sun, and our glory is but the reflection of God's glory. Yet the world sometimes comes between the sun and the moon, and her light is turned into darkness. So, I fear, the world often comes between us and God, and our glory is turned into shame. But beyond death's gloom no world can ever obstruct the eternal glory. It will forever and forever shine upon these cold, barren souls of ours—these vessels of mercy—and the clay will be forgotten in the light, the desolation hidden in the glory.

And another thought rushes upon us here. Who ever thinks of the utter darkness, the silent, lifeless, barren wastes, the cold, dry, dreary deserts of the moon when, ablaze with the light of the hidden sun, she sails across our wintry sky, or sinks to rest behind our summer western clouds? Still she is cold, barren, dead. And so are we. Very beautiful we shall be in our Father's home, but it will be in His beauty, in His glory. We shall be nothing—only vessels of mercy. Remember this then. What we are in relation to God here we shall be hereafter. Our life will be His life. Our joy will be His joy. Our wealth will be His wealth. And in this very fact the eternity of our happiness will rest. As God's word cannot fail, neither can His power. We can depend upon that.

And when He shall make known to us the riches of His glory how speechless we shall stand in His presence! We shall need the new song then to be put into our mouths. No song of earth will express our joy. What will all the past be—or what the future in that glorious present? What the sin, the shame, the grief of this world beneath those rays of golden light! All will be forgotten then. One grand, eternal, ever present glory will be to us the consummation of all things. We shall see God, and to see Him is all that heart can wish for. We shall know then that we never could have earned, never could have attained to such joy. We shall know then that God has done it all. We shall know that it was He that led us and controlled our steps. To Him be all the glory!

One word more. I have spoken of doubts. Oh, what doubting hearts ours are! We are always questioning God's promises. We never seem to be able to take Him at His word. Perhaps many will say that the assurance given in our text depends upon conditions. True, but only upon one—not our attainments—but upon the fact of our being vessels of mercy. Upon those who have found mercy God will show His glory. But am I a vessel of mercy? some one will ask. Oh, that we might all put this solemn question to ourselves! Let me ask, do you think you need mercy? Have you done anything that you feel has placed you under God's condemnation? Would you ask for mercy? If so, then mercy is yours. "Him that cometh unto Me I will in no wise cast out." There is an assurance for you from God. Feel your need of mercy, go to Him for it—cry out, as the poor publican did, "God be merciful to me a sinner"—and mercy is yours. Go to God as an empty vessel and He will fill you with mercy. You will go from that blessed presence a vessel of mercy. Did I say "go"? No, you will remain there. You will go out no more. The gracious influence that brought you there will keep you there. You cannot possibly doubt that. Only be as nothing. Look at your sin, and not at the good deeds you have done. They are nothing, but oh! the sin, how deep, how black! Do you doubt it? Think of God's righteousness and love, and you can doubt that point no longer. We have seen the winter's snow upon the ground. How white and beautiful! Spotless and pure we say. And so it looks, but as it fell it gathered in the air minute particles of dust and smoke—so minute that we cannot see them, and they lie hid in that mass of seeming purity. Melt the snow and we find dirty water. And so many a life seems pure, many a heart seems free from sin, but oh! melt that life, that heart, in the fire of God's love, and the dark corruption will be manifest, the foul taint be seen. There is the sin. If we know it, then is it not because God has revealed it to us? And there is the mercy hiding, forgiving, forgetting the sin. Oh, that we may all realize this blessed truth! Oh, that every unforgiven one reading this sermon may fall down at His feet and leave it all with Him! Oh, that we may leave everything with Him! He will save. He will guide. He will keep. He will never leave nor forsake them that trust Him. All is and ever will be in His hand. Let us rest, then, our soul, our all, upon Him. His purpose concerning us is eternal, sure and gracious. It is " That He might make known the riches of His glory on the vessels of mercy, which He had afore prepared unto glory."

SERMON X.

THE LIFE OF CHRIST.

GALATIANS II. 20.--"I live; yet not I, but Christ liveth in me."

THE perpetual presence of Christ with His people is assured them by the Master's last words to the Apostles, " Lo I am with you alway." Wherever they might be, or in whatever circumstances placed, their Lord was with them. Whether it were in prayer or worship—" where two or three are gathered together in my name there am I in the midst of them ;" or in distress and tribulation —" when thou passest through the waters I will be with thee ;" or in doubt and anxiety—" I will guide thee with Mine eye: "—in all the changes and wants of life the promise ever was, " I will never leave thee nor forsake thee." So that God's people in view of this assured presence might say with David " I will fear no evil: for Thou art with me," and be bold in the fact that "the Lord is nigh unto all them that call upon Him, to all that call upon Him in truth."

But the Apostle in my text leads us on to a higher and more glorious truth than even this. He declares that Christ is our very life. " I live : yet not I, but Christ liveth in me." There is something more than mere presence. There is indwelling life.

So that Christ is not only with His people, guarding, guiding and hearing them, but He is in them—He is the living principle, the actual source of spiritual life. Let us, dear reader, look a little at the nature of this INDWELLING PRESENCE AND LIFE OF CHRIST.

And the *first* thing we may observe of it is, that it is a PERSONAL LIFE.

Life could not be otherwise than personal. Yet many people speak of spiritual life as general. They partake of it in general with the whole Church. They would rather say "we live" than "I live"—rather look upon the whole as living than a part. The consequence of this is, Christ is no more to us individually than a king is to the great mass of his subjects. They indeed feel the benefit of his just laws and efficient administration, but they know nothing of him personally. Christ must be far more to us than this. He must not be merely a general influence but a personal life, so that each one of us may say, " Christ liveth in me." This is the doctrine which is taught us in the Sacrament of the Lord's Supper ; there is an individual participation of the elements which symbolize our spiritual sustenance—an individual commemoration of the sacrifice of Christ's death.

The personal life of Christ in His people must be taken in a literal sense. We may not rob our text of its plain and natural force. All mankind derives its animal life from Adam. The vital germ planted in him by the Creator is diffused throughout the whole human family. The life which is now in us was once in Adam, so that we may say in a sense that Adam lives in us. Now if Adam's life in us be actual and real, Christ's far more so : for Adam is dead but Christ is living—Adam's life is transmitted to us through many generations, but Christ's by immediate, personal contact with the soul. To animate a mass of matter so that it shall live as man, the life of Adam must be imparted to it : to animate the soul so that it may live unto God the life of Christ must be imparted to it ; so that in the body we have an animal life and in the soul a spiritual life. This is the meaning of our Lord's words to Nicodemus, "Ye must be born again." The first birth, that of the body, from Adam, must be supplemented by the second birth, that of the soul, from above. The natural man may then say : "I live in the life transmitted to me from Adam," and the spiritual man may say with St. Paul, "I live ; yet not I, but Christ liveth in me."

The question may be asked how is this spiritual life imparted to the soul ? An answer is very simple. It is by the mind. The soul is reached by the mind. An intelligent appreciation of the truth as it is in Jesus—a mental grasping of the fact of His work and our condition—is the channel by which life is given to the soul. The reason must be exercised.

Hence the scripture says "We are born again by the word of God" because that word is addressed to our mind, and through it, by the help of the Holy Spirit, reaches our soul. In this sense it is called "quick *i.e.* living and powerful." And this being the mode of imparting life it is evident that it must be personally apprehended. The individual himself must "lay hold on eternal life." "The effectual fervent prayer of a righteous man availeth much" for the benefit of his brother, but his faith availeth nothing for the justification of another. So that in prayer we may say "Our Father" but in faith it is "I believe." A personal faith leading each one of us individually to the Saviour is the secret of this personal life. There must be a personal death unto sin, so that there may be a personal resurrection unto righteousness. With this personal life the Christian may speak of himself and the Redeemer to the exclusion of everyone else. St. Paul could say "I am the chief of sinners," "but I obtained mercy." There is no one between us and the Master. It is a close relationship. We are one with Him, because His life is our life. Our dead souls live because He has given them life. It is well for us to see that we have this indwelling personal life. Am I "a new creature in Christ Jesus?" Can I say with St. Paul, "Christ liveth in me." If we cannot speak of this life as ours, then we know it not. If we have no personal interest in Christ, He will have no personal interest in us.

But the life of Christ in us besides being personal, is in the *second* place DEVELOPING.

It grows in the soul. At first it is but a germ, but it progresses on and on to perfection. It is strong or weak according as it is nourished and strengthened by the means of grace which God has provided for our spiritual food. The young convert will not be as able to resist sin and temptation as the older and maturer Christian. But however weak or strong our life may be it is a life that may be felt. We must know that we are living. We are conscious of it in its results. The result of the life of Christ in us is holiness and sanctification. "If Christ be in you," says St. Paul, "the body is dead because of sin." The grace of God which is in us teacheth us "that denying ungodliness and worldly lusts, we should live soberly, righteously and godly, in this present world," and St. John declares that "whosoever is born of. God doth not commit sin: for His seed remaineth in him: and he cannot sin because he is born of God." "The wisdom that is from above is first pure, then peaceable, gentle and easy to be intreated, full of mercy and good fruits, without partiality and without hypocrisy." There will be a general disinclination to sin on the part of one who is living in Christ. This is the best test we can have that we are truly the children of God. We may not know the form and essence of spiritual life any more than we know the form and essence of natural life, but we discern it by its effects. We know whether we delight in the things pertaining unto life or in the things of this world. The life itself is indeed "hid with Christ in God"—a veil is drawn over it because we are unable to behold its glory—but the light of that life should "so shine before men that they may see our good works and glorify our Father which is in heaven."

I am not saying impossible things. A holy life is demanded of us. That life we shall certainly live if we are born again. I do not say we shall never fall or that we shall be proof against temptation. But I do say that holiness will reign over sin, that the spiritual life will be supreme above the natural. As that life gets stronger so will it be more victorious. We are to grow in grace. The life of Christ in us will develope and make itself felt more and more day by day. Sin will hide it and taint its glory, but gradually it will become bright and clear as the noonday.

You have seen the full moon rise on a warm summer evening. How blood-red it looks as it looms on the misty horizon! But as it rises it gradually becomes brighter and more silver-like, till in the mid-heavens it sails across the starry space untainted by aught of earth, majestic in its quiet and silent beauty. So the Christian at the beginning of his career is coloured with earth's darkening mists, but as he rises higher and higher towards heaven he shines with a clearer light, he is touched with a greater glory!

Now we have all of us some talent which the Lord has committed to our charge. It is our duty to use that talent. We must not hide it because it is a single one and we see our neighbour with ten such. This is what many do. But the life of Christ in us urges us on to activity. We cannot with that life be idle. It must show itself. As well say that the bright sun cannot be seen in a clear, unclouded sky, as that the spiritual life in a man will not be manifest. In whatever sphere our lot may be cast, our talent, be it little or be it great, will be developed and brought out. Wherever there is life there will be movement and progression. There are babes in Christ and there are grown men. Some will be capable of great achievements and others only of small ones. The little rill up in the mountains cannot do much more than wend its way to the plain. But the farther it runs the greater and stronger it grows, till by and by it can turn the great mill wheel, and farther on it can bear mighty ships upon its bosom. So with us in our Christian life. Small indeed at first, but as we flow on we grow greater and stronger till finally that which would kill us in our youth becomes a thing of nought to us in our manhood.

An acorn is sown in the earth. It springs up a tiny sprout that a careless step from a passer-by might crush. It grows till it becomes a sapling; then a young tree, and the birds make their home in its branches. By and by it becomes a giant forest oak, able to shelter a multitude beneath its broad green boughs. The life that was in the acorn has developed it into the great tree. So the germ of eternal life in the soul. It developes it. It enlarges it. It strengthens it. That which at one time was so weak that it might have been blasted forever had it not been cared for, is now strong enough to withstand the wild tempest, and able itself to overshadow and protect weaker ones from the burning heat of temptation and sin.

It is for us to see that the life we have is developing within us. If we are not growing—if we are not getting stronger day by day—there is something wrong. Either we have not the real life in us, or we are not nourishing it, as is our duty. It is not loud professions that testify of our life; nor is it a mechanical performance of the outward duties of religion; but it is the surrender of the will to God—the intense desire to serve Him—to draw nearer and nearer to Him. We may be very weak; we may not have the power to attain to that ideal which the ardent longing of the soul sets before us,—do we ever in the natural life realize the ambition of an aspiring mind?—but the very fact that there are longings, that there is an ambition, is an evidence of life. We are dissatisfied with self—another proof of life, for death knows no dissatisfaction; and we fear we have no life. But the test of all is in the inclination toward God, in the desire to avoid sin. I do not say we shall always go straight and right. I have stood on a high hill overlooking a great plain. A broad river wound its way amid the corn fields and meadows, and through the green woods. It did not run straight. It twisted and turned, now to the right, ere long to the left; and at one place it leaped over a high dam. But, in spite of all this, there was a general inclination in those waters to flow to the sea; and so their progress was onward. So with us. We may perhaps sometimes fall from the straight line; but notwithstanding that, our lives will have the general inclination to flow heavenward—our progress will be on and on to God. Do we find such to be the case in our experience? Are we going onward, developing and growing all the time? It is well we should think of this ere it be too late; for the indwelling life of Christ is one which is developing and growing more and more into the measure of the perfect man.

But, in the *third* place, besides being personal and developing, it is a TRIUMPHANT LIFE.

It is a matter of great comfort to us to know that

this life never dies. He who can say, "Christ liveth in me," will never taste of spiritual death. I believe that we may indeed lapse into sin, but we will rise again; sin cannot kill our life. This is proved by the very term applied to this life. It is called everlasting. Christ saith, "Whosoever eateth My flesh and drinketh My blood," that is to say, whosoever receives life and nourishment from Me, "hath eternal life." Mark the word "hath"—it is present, not future—he has it now. But if he could forfeit that life—if sin could kill it—it would not be eternal. Besides, as our text says, "I live; yet not I, but Christ liveth in me." The life we have in us is the life of Christ; and we know that "Christ being raised from the dead, dieth no more; death hath no more dominion over Him." So He says to His people, "Because I live, ye shall live also." To say that we who are born again can die a second time unto the Lord, is as much as to say that the life we have is not eternal, and that it is not the life of Christ. It is to give the lie to those solemn words of our Blessed Lord—" My sheep hear My voice, and I know them, and they follow Me; and I give unto them eternal life; and they shall never perish, neither shall any one pluck them out of My hand." The "never" in that passage is as emphatic as the Greek can make it. It is a declaration that no amount of interpretation can destroy. We poor helpless sheep shall live for ever. The life we have in us is a life that can triumph over sin and death—a life that is divine and eternal in its very nature. "I live; yet not I, but Christ liveth in me."

The strength and assurance that this can give to the child of God is very great. It gives us a certainty of safety. It may not perhaps be our privilege to feel this. That is another thing. Many people are safe in Christ though they do not feel or realize it. It is His life which is in us, not our own life. It is His hand holding us, and not our hand holding Him. What then have we to fear? Shall sin tear us from Him? Shall sin destroy His life which is in us? "I am persuaded," says St. Paul, "that neither death nor life, nor angels, nor principalities, nor powers, nor things present, nor things to come, nor height, nor depth, nor any other creature shall be able to separate us from the love of God, which is in Christ Jesus our Lord." The life of Christ in man can triumph over sin.

How often, when we have been overcome with temptation, we have feared lest the sin had severed us for ever from God! We have gone astray like lost sheep—at the best we are but miserable sinners —and when we think of this, we wonder, nay, we doubt whether we are indeed God's people—whether the life that is in us can survive all attacks. But we have enough to show us that, in spite of our shortcomings, we can never die the second death. Sin may be strong but we shall naturally fight against it and withstand it. We may be wounded in the fight; we may fall on the field; but we shall not be killed. Sin cannot a second time kill the Lord of life. And if sin cannot do this, neither can death. We may be sure that the life in us can triumph over the great enemy of our race. And this is the great test of its strength. In that terrible moment nought but this life can be of service to us. Whatever we may have now, we shall want nothing but Christ then. He will be all to us then. Death may lay its hand upon the worn-out tabernacle of clay—this body may seem as though it were ready to break up into dust—but the life which has hitherto been our own—our personal life, the life which has developed within us, shall then be triumphant—and we shall be free! In the very darkness of the valley of the shadow of death, we may exclaim, "I live; yet not I, but Christ liveth in me."

My dear reader, the subject before us is a very important one. The thought must come home to you as well as to me—" Have I this life ? Am I living in Christ Jesus?" Let us meet that solemn question with all honesty and sincerity. Am I or am I not a child of God? I ask not whether you are a professing Christian; nor do I ask whether you have been baptized. The life I have been speaking of is not in profession, nor is it in baptism. But I ask you, as I ask my own soul, can you say, not we live, but "I live"? Are you conscious of a power within you that is developing your soul and leading you on to God? Has that power in you been triumphant over sin and temptation? It may be you are one who is walking in the noontide of God's presence; or perhaps you are in the midnight darkness of sin; and, in either case, can give a clear "yes," or "no." But there are others who are in the twilight—standing afar off, yet looking eagerly for the dawning of the clear day. These can give no answer. It trembles on their lips, and dies there amid the deep heart doubts. What can I say to such? They are the waiting ones. For what are they waiting? Is it for the fuller manifestation of Christ? Is it to be drawn closer and closer to him? Ah, there is life! The dead soul wants no Christ—the dead soul wants no communion with Him. The sign of life is in that very twilight position. Oh that they might look to God —waiting on Him, trusting in His promises! In God's own time, all will be clear. The life in them will be triumphant over doubt, it will lead them to the bright day, it will enable each one to say, "I live; yet not I, but Christ liveth in me."

May this be our experience; may we indeed find Christ precious to our souls. If we want life, He says, "I am the life." If we have life, still He says, "I am that life." We are nothing; He is everything. We are dead, it is Christ that liveth in us.

Oh, glorious truth! "We dwell in Christ, and Christ in us; we are one with Christ, and Christ with us;" so that Christ and His people being thus united to God, God is all, and in all. Not merely is His presence with us, but His life is in us. May it be ours to realize that life, and to say with the Apostle, "I live; yet not I, but Christ liveth in me!"

SERMON XI.

THE POWER OF CHRIST'S NAME.

St. John xvi. 23.—" Verily, verily, I say unto you, whatsoever ye shall ask the Father in My name, He will give it you."

THAT there is a Supreme Being, who made and governs the world, is a fact which the great majority of men in all ages have admitted. They may, indeed, have differed in their conception of that Being, but few denied the existence of such a Being. There is another fact also generally held, and that is that man is dependent upon this God—that he owes Him submission, and derives from Him not only life, but everything that concerns that life or supports it· Man's helplessness and God's power were and are thus recognized by the great mass of mankind.

From these two facts followed a third—the necessity of some communication between this Supreme Being and the creatures dependent upon Him. And it is a singular thing that the world at large conceived God and man, though linked together, to be at enmity with each other. And so in approaching Him, as of necessity they felt they must, the ancients took with them some propitiatory sacrifice or offering whereby they might appease His wrath and obtain His blessing. If we look back to antiquity, we find this idea carried out literally and constantly. Blood was shed, and some attempt made to expiate sin and remove the existing alienation in order to institute that communication which was involved in the fact of God's supremacy and man's dependency.

Now these three points thus held by the heathen world had in them a great deal of truth. To be sure, they were not understood as the enlightened Jews understood them. To them this great God had revealed Himself. The relation they maintained towards Him was amply set forth by inspired prophets and divinely instructed priests. A way of access was pointed out by which they might reach Him. The men to whom Jesus was speaking when He uttered the words of my text knew of these important truths. They knew that prayer was the road to the throne of grace. But they did not know that the old propitiatory sacrifice was no longer necessary; that they needed something far more efficacious to bring an answer to their prayers.

The Lord Jesus Christ, in the passage before us for consideration, taught the disciples this lesson: "Whatsoever ye shall ask the Father in My name, He will give it you." "In My name," that is to say, the mention of His name in our prayers will procure for us that which we seek. He is the sacrifice we must offer in our communication with the God to whom we desire to be reconciled, or of whom we desire a blessing. This is a truth which the heathen world did not know, and which it was the mission of Christianity to reveal. It brings to our attention the great power of the name of Jesus.

We have some idea given us of this power when the Apostle tells us "that at the name of Jesus every knee should bow, of things in heaven, and things in earth, and things under the earth." Such is the honour the Father hath given Him that He hath put all things under His feet. The fame of His glory and might and dominion has gone out to the remotest corners of the vast universe, and all things acknowledge Him to be their Lord. His very name receives its homage. We have an illustration analogous to this in everyday life. The name of an earthly sovereign—pre-eminently that of an oriental monarch—carries with it authority and respect wherever it goes. Travellers in the east tell us that the wild Arab is stayed in his purpose of plunder when the firman is produced with the Sultan's name attached. The bare name calls for the reverence of every faithful Mahometan, just as the name of our own gracious Queen calls for the honour and obedience of all her subjects. But more powerful among men than the name of an earthly king is the name of our great King of kings, the Lord Jesus Christ. Millions here below, and untold millions above, bow the knee before Him. God hath given Him a name which is above every name. To the farthest bounds of the great creation—through heaven and earth and hell

—by angels, men and devils—that name is uttered with adoring love, or breathed with helpless dependence, or whispered with despairing fear. It is the one name that has supreme authority. With that name upon his lips, Peter could look upon the lame man lying at the gate of the temple and say, "Silver and gold have I none; but such as I have give I thee; in the name of Jesus Christ of Nazareth, rise up and walk;" and before the rulers of the people and the elders of Israel he could declare, "that by the name of Jesus Christ of Nazareth, whom ye crucified, whom God raised from the dead, even by Him doth this man stand before you whole." And, indeed, the sum and substance of the Apostles' teaching was that "there is none other name under heaven given among men whereby we must be saved."

Such is the power of the name of Christ above all the names of the men of earth. I might mention the name of a Nelson, and it would thrill the heart of many with the remembrance of his bravery; the name of a Shakespeare would delight as many more; and the mention of Jonathan would recall his intense friendship for his rival, the future king of Israel. But these names have only a limited power. They are eminent names, but they have no power in distress or disease or death. They are then forgotten and fade away before the glory of the name of Jesus. That name is far more to the bereaved and afflicted, to the sorrowful and heavy laden, to the tempest-tossed and dying, than all other names that man has ever breathed. And if to us it is so much, what is it to His Father, the Lord God Almighty? What is it to Him, of whom He is the very brightness of His glory, the express image of His person?

I cannot fathom the mystery of the connection between the Father and the Son. I cannot grasp that which is so far beyond the bare conception of man. But I remember how God spoke of Him by the mouth of Isaiah as His elect in whom His soul delighted. I remember how, at the baptism at Jordan, a voice proclaimed from heaven, "This is My beloved Son in whom I am well pleased." I remember the declaration of the Apostles before the Jewish Council: "Him hath God exalted with His right hand to be a Prince and a Saviour." And I know that these are not words without meaning. They touch upon that wonderful relationship which we can never understand. But they are enough to show me that the Lord Jesus is indeed very precious in the sight of the Father. He is the Son of His love, the Beginning of the creation of God, the Pre-eminent One to whom all power is given both in heaven and in earth. And such being the case, the power of His name in approaching the great and eternal God is unrivalled, and untouched with the spirit of failure. With that name, then, I need no other offering to appease God's wrath or gain access to the throne of grace; I want no sacrifice, no more shedding of blood, for the promise of the King of righteousness standeth sure: "Whatsoever ye shall ask the Father in My name, He will give it you." A name which the Supreme Being loves and honours, and a name which we, His creatures, obey and reverence, is just the name for us to have upon our lips when we seek for reconciliation or implore His blessing.

If we want an illustration of the power of a name in procuring favours from others, we have an abundance in our common experience. I am going a journey, and a friend comes to me and says: "If you choose to call on so-and-so, in such a place, and mention my name, I am sure he will be glad to see you and to help you." A letter of introduction is brought to me by a stranger; its entire strength and value lie in the name subscribed to it. I read a story somewhere of an officer who, when dying in a foreign land, called to his bedside one whose interest he had very much at heart, and bid him, when he returned home, to go to his father's house, and tell him that he was with his son on his death-bed, and for his sake desired his help. The officer died, and his friend went home, and to the father's house, and with difficulty obtained access to him. He was a proud, haughty man, and he treated the unknown stranger at first coldly and sternly. But when the soldier dropped the name of his son the father's heart was touched, his tone was changed, and he seized him warmly by the hand. The name of the lost one had a power over him that nothing else could possibly have had.

And similar to this, though infinitely more certain of success, is the power of the name of Jesus over the heart of God. There is the returning penitent pleading for mercy and forgiveness. That sin-stained soul is not worthy of coming into God's presence. Its iniquities are deserving of anything but pardon. And the sinner knows this. He does not ask God to save him because he is worth saving. He does not ask God to save him because he has done or ever can do anything to entitle him to such a favour. Were he to do so, God would not answer. But he asks that he may be saved for Jesus' sake, and immediately the arm of justice is stayed, and the impending wrath is averted. By the mention of that name he draws attention from himself—his own dark self—to Him who is the chiefest among ten thousand and the altogether lovely; he draws around himself the spotless robe of Christ's righteousness: he hides his sins in the crimson blood of the Atonement. And so will all who come to God. Whatever mercy we want, whatever blessing we implore—whether we are in sickness, adversity or sorrow, or in prosperity and joy, that is the name we plead, that is the name upon which we rest all our hopes.

When the Jewish high-priest entered the Holy of Holies, into the presence of God, he was obliged to hide himself within the clouds of incense, and to sprinkle the blood of the sacrifice about the mercy seat. But when we exercise our priestly office and go before God, we surround ourselves with the incense of Christ's glorious name and bring to God's remembrance His blood—the blood of the New Covenant—shed for us. And our prayer thus offered is never offered in vain. It may be lisped by the little child or muttered by the aged and dying saint; it may be spoken by the blinded sinner or by the valiant Christian; but if it be in the name of Jesus, it will be sure to draw down a blessing, it will be sure to bring together the Creator and the creature. The Lord Jesus Christ stands between us and God. He is the centre of our adoration, the centre of God's love. God sees us only acceptably through Him, and through Him only can we fearlessly see God. And, therefore, we have assurance that whatsoever we shall ask the Father in His name, He will give it us. We have through Him that access to God which the whole heathen world struggled in the darkness to attain.

But the Lord Jesus, besides giving us permission to use His name, and assuring us of the certainty of its success, has given us a most unbounded and unlimited authority. " Whatsoever ye shall ask." It makes no difference what may be the wants and desires of His people, He will be responsible for them.

He loves to bear our petitions to the throne of grace. He loves to have His name used freely and without reserve. There is a great advantage in this. Were a man to give me an unqualified right to use his name at his banker's, or among his friends, whenever I needed anything, be it little or be it much, be it often or be it seldom, I should be far better off than were he to limit me to times and occasions and circumstances. The Lord Jesus has given us that absolute privilege—"whatsoever,"—anything, everything, without limit or restraint, if asked in His name, we shall have. I may go to Him every day, every hour, every moment, yea, I may never cease my importunity, but He is not tired. I may draw down blessings all the time, both great and small, but His treasury is not emptied, nor His patience exhausted. I may utter His name with my lips of sin, but His love for the sinner is not impaired, nor the permission He has given withdrawn. The "whatsoever" in the text covers all, and shields every one who chooses to come to God through Christ.

There are times when we are in great distress of conscience through temptation and sin. Our souls are then overwhelmed within us. Darkness encompasses us round about, and the sense of our unworthiness grows greater and greater. We may have been in this state before. We remember how repeatedly God has delivered us, but now we feel that He will deliver us no more. We feel that the end has come, and we shall be rejected from His presence forever. What child of God is there that has not again and again been plunged in this terrible distress? But the "whatsoever" comes to our rescue! "Whatsoever ye shall ask the Father in my name, He will give it you." Ask Him for deliverance. "Out of the depths have I cried unto thee, O Lord: Lord hear my voice; let thine ears be attentive to the voice of my supplications." And the answer is "Let not your heart be troubled: ye believe in God, believe also in Me." In such an experience as that let us believe in the power of the name of Jesus,—let us believe in His full and glorious promises, and we shall be saved!

Again, there are times of persecution for His name's sake and the profession of the Gospel. If we would follow Christ, depend upon it we must go through great tribulations. No man can walk in the narrow way without bearing the cross and carrying the shame. And as long as there is a godly person left in the world, that world will destroy itself rather than let him rest in peace. This is indeed very hard. It is difficult for flesh and blood to bear. And oftentimes we faint beneath the heavy burden. It is not the wilderness, the prison, the dungeon, nor even the martyr's fire that expresses all this tribulation. The laugh, the sneer, and the taunt, the evil word and the unkind action—these are things that try the soul. They cast us down and make us feel our weakness. We need our Father's strength then. We need to look up to one who is mighty to help. And we have our Master's "whatsoever ye shall ask" rising around us like some mighty bulwark of hope protecting us from the darts of the evil one. We want comfort and strength and wisdom. "Ask and ye shall receive." The name of Jesus will procure for us whatsoever we have need of!

Again, there are times of deep sorrow when we are sorely afflicted. Death may have entered our little circle of relations or friends, and hurried some loved one away out of our sight. Or the misconduct of a near and trusted friend—perhaps a father, a brother, a husband, a wife, a child—has made our heart bleed with grief. Or business may have gone wrong with us, and we find ourselves irretrievably involved to the jeopardy of our honour and hope, and to the almost certain fact of our ruin. These are trials of no ordinary magnitude. They are verily sore afflictions. They may well make us water our couch with tears. And the special temptation accompanying them—for every trial has its own temptation—is that they are not things worthy of being brought before God. Were we going to martyrdom, then we might call upon God, but these every-day affairs we think are beneath His notice. And yet it is just in these common events that we need help as much as in the greater and more important. We want something to heal the wounded and broken heart. We want something to dry up the streams of sorrow. And it is a lying devil that would tell us we cannot have that something. "God is our refuge and strength, a very present help in trouble." "Whatsoever ye shall ask," says Jesus—and surely that "whatsoever" is enough. If I want comfort beside the grave, if I want the conversion of an erring friend, if I want encouragement in adversity—whatsoever it may be, if I ask for it in the name of Jesus, the Father will give it me. The promise is surer than the everlasting hills: "Call upon me in the day of trouble, and I will deliver thee, and thou shalt glorify me." When He could save the Israelites by making a way for them through the sea, when he could send them down bread from heaven and water out of the stony rock, when he could rescue Daniel in the lion's den, the three Hebrew children in the fiery furnace, Peter from Herod's prison, I have no doubt He will do for me all that I have need of. "Whatsoever ye shall ask the Father in my name, He will give it you."

Have we availed ourselves of this glorious promise? Have we sought to come to God by Him who is the living way? Do we know how dependent we are upon Him? Surely we need Him in all the scenes of life. Do we now embrace the invitation to go unto Him? Is the name of Jesus ever on our lips when we draw nigh to God?

There comes a day to all when we shall stand in need of God's grace and mercy more than at any other time. When we are passing through the dark valley of the shadow of death, on our way to the home of His presence, we shall need the light to guide and the strength to sustain. Faith will then be tested to the uttermost. Satan will then bend all his powers to prevent the meeting of the Saviour and the sinner. Earthly stays and earthly supports will pass away and be forever lost, and we shall go down to the river's brink and into the cold waters alone. Then will the name of Jesus be full of power. No cloud, no fear, no sin shall touch us with that name welling up from the depths of our redeemed and ransomed soul. That name, though fainter than a whisper, shall pierce the gloom, and reach the Father's ear. That name, though tremblingly uttered, shall still the raging cry of demons, and draw the legions of the mighty angels to the rescue. Away beyond the night, away beyond the swelling flood, that name shall be but breathed, and heaven's eternal gates shall open wide, and, through the shining streets, amid the music of celestial hosts, we shall draw near the palace of the King—to His very presence—to go out no more for ever. And in that glorious welcome and that fond embrace the only word will be "Jesus—Jesus—none but Jesus!"

Beloved reader, would you be there where He reigns a Prince for ever? Would you see Him as He is? It may be yours. We may be one with God. We may approach that throne, though heathen, Jew, and all mankind, knew not the way. It is by Jesus. He is the way, there is none other. He calls us to Him—you and me, whosoever will. To each of us He says, " Behold, I stand at the door, and knock: if any man hear my voice and open the door, I will come in to him, and will sup with him, and he with me." Oh let us open unto Him! Let us learn the name of Jesus now, so that when the day of necessity comes it may have no strange sound! Let us make this key to God's presence—this sceptre of might and favour—this everlasting sacrifice, our very own! In this life of sin and sorrow and death we want a Saviour, we want a Father, and all their love and care and strength. We need them every hour. If we would be happy, we must have them God tells us how all may be ours. Ask—pray—pray without ceasing, pray for everything, but only in the name of the Lord Jesus. There is no other name, no other plea, no other offering. " Whatsoever ye shall ask the Father in my name, He will give it you." That is all, that is everything. Take the name of Jesus with you, and whatsoever ye shall ask, it shall be yours.

May God make this Saviour precious to us, that in Him we may have boldness and access with confidence to the throne of the great Jehovah, to the presence of the Supreme Ruler, the mighty God of all the earth : and this we ask in the name and for the sake of our ever-glorious Mediator, the Lord Jesus Christ.

SERMON XII.

THE GOOD GIFTS OF GOD.

St. Matthew vii. 11.—"If ye then, being evil, know how to give good gifts unto your children, how much more shall your Father, which is in heaven, give good things to them that ask Him?"

THAT man is full of sin is evident not only from the declarations of the Word of God, but from our own experience and observation. In every sense of the term, we are evil. And this evil has injured and impaired our powers beyond measure. It has killed the soul. It has weakened our ability to think and to love, and has limited the range of our reason to a very narrow sphere. But notwithstanding all this, there is wisdom and affection remaining sufficient to enable us to give good gifts unto our children. Corrupt as our natures are and full of innate selfishness, we are yet full of love for our offspring, and full of a desire to feed and care for them. Experience teaches us what is good for them and what evil, and we instinctively do our uttermost to keep them from the evil and provide them with the good. And with our weak and limited wisdom, we so act towards them as to bring them from helplessness to strength, from the bud of infancy to the blossom of youth.

But if this be true of us—if we know something

of the *how* to give and the *when* to give—what of God, of Him who is infinite in all things,—in His wisdom, His love, and His might? Shall He not know better than any earthly parent how to give good gifts to His children? Such is the teaching of our text: " If ye then, being evil, know how to give good gifts unto your children, how much more shall your Father, which is in heaven, give good things to them that ask Him?"

And there is something very comforting, to which the heart instinctively clings, at the very first reading of the text. It is to the Fatherhood of God. The Lord Jesus calls Him our Father; on another occasion He taught us to pray to Him as such; and the view given to us of God throughout the Scriptures confirms the incidental statement made in this place. By creation and by redemption, by generation and by adoption, He has made us His sons and His daughters. And in the glorious fact that we are all God's children by creation, and may all become His children by adoption, we see much to encourage and strengthen us. We know that if He is our Father, He must love us; and more than that, His love must be perfect and infinite, for there can be no flaw in the character or attributes of God. And, as a matter of fact, we find that love encircling us like some boundless ocean encircling the rocky island; every way we look there is love; if we launch out into the deep, we cannot find its limit, we cannot reach the point where the sky and the sea seem to meet. Day by day God cares for us, provides and protects us. Every moment that comes to us, and leaves as soon as it comes, brings with it some rich and undeserved mercy. Awake or asleep, day and night, in joy or in sorrow, still God remains our Father, and His love—the everlasting, the unchanging love—like the flowing rays of the kindly sun, shines upon us and bears to us blessings beyond number, yea, as David said, "If I should count them they are more in number than the sand." Oh, how the heart loves to rest, as it were, upon this blessed truth! It is a precious relationship to think of. It makes every fibre of the soul to thrill with joy when we remember that every creature under the broad heavens—every child of Adam—is also a child of God. He is their Father. He watches over us as a father watches over the child of his love. The Lord Jesus struck a most wonderful chord when He spoke of the Fatherhood of God, when He told us that this great God was even our Father.

And, springing out of this Fatherhood, arises the truth brought more prominently before us in our text. Christ speaks of the good things our Father gives to us, His children. It is a father's duty and a father's pleasure to give good gifts to his own, but we know that in spite of our boasted experience, we often make mistakes in giving. Some of us are apt to give to our little ones that which is not good for them. It may be we feel it hard to thwart their inclinations, and rather than have them want, we give them their desire at all risks. It is wrong to do so—very wrong. It is a great mistake, and we know it. God makes no such mistakes. His wisdom is unerring in this as in everything else.

This is an important fact to bear in mind. We often think God errs though we may not say as much. There is not a man or woman in the world that is entirely without longings for something they do not possess. They may have worked for that something—struggled for it through long years—and yet have never received it. And if they have longed for it very ardently, they are apt to murmur somewhat when they see others receive the prize for which they have not striven perhaps half as much. Why should God give it to them and not to us? they are very likely to ask. But God had his own reason.

There are people who would have riches, who work for them, but they never get them. There are others who aim at high places of position and trust, but they are withheld from them all the days of their life. And yet these very individuals may have been truly God's children, may have asked Him continually to bless them according to His will, and still their heart's desire remains unsatisfied. And it was in the very fact that they feared God, and would submit themselves to Him, that they never received either riches or honour. God knew that such things would not be good for them, and so, in His loving wisdom, He withheld them.

Let me give an illustration. There were two young men in college, both studying for the ministry. To be sent forth to preach the Gospel was the height of their ambition. They knew that God could place them in no higher position in this world than to make them ambassadors to their fallen and dying brethren. They knew that the humblest servant in that divinely-instituted ministry stood in the kingdom of God higher than kings or the great men of the earth—yea, higher than the angels of heaven. And they aspired to that office. They prayed for it with a noble faith and constant devotion. They had no other desire than that, and yet only one of them was taken. The good thing which the other longed for, and worked for, was never given to him, and he was obliged to serve God in a lower, though none the less honourable, sphere. It was hard for him to see the justice of the Providence that led to the frustration of all his hopes. He saw it afterwards. By and bye he could thank his heavenly Father for withholding from him what, in his case, would have been no good gift.

There are multitudes of instances such as that. In fact, the company of disappointed hopers is very great. In every condition of life there are plenty to be found who have an idea that their prayers have all been answered backwards. They have prayed for health, and yet God has led them to the bed of sickness and affliction. They have prayed for prosperity, and yet nothing came but failure and disappointment. Instead of a smooth road through the bright sunshine, it has been a rough, almost untrodden track through the dark night and storm and danger. They saw held out before them a cup which they thought contained the very wine of joy; but, lo, it was filled with the bitter gall of grief and sorrow. Around them were homes full of happiness, but *their* hearths were desolate by the ravages of death. There are men surrounded by warm friends, but *they* are friendless and forsaken. Oh, it is very hard to bear all this! Everything they get seems to be an evil thing—a cross rather than a crown. Could God have forsaken them? Could He have forgotten His promise to give them the good things? Why is the bread withheld—the pleasures in which others seem to revel? God knows. Depend upon it, He is not withholding anything from us without a reason. We may not know it. "What thou knowest not now thou shalt know hereafter." God sees that the thing which we would desire is not good for us. It might harm us if we had it. It may be much better for us to be wearied before we are given rest. It may be much better for us to feel the hardships and disappointments of this life, in order that we may the better enjoy the peace and bliss of the better world. All these things are in God's hands. And we need to realize that fact. If He be our Father, as we know He is, then we must believe that He does all things well. When an earthly father withholds from his child that which the child so ardently craves for, it is for some good purpose, and we know it is. Why, then, have we not the same faith in reference to our heavenly Father? Is He not far better able to tell what is good for us than any father of earth? Infinite love and infinite wisdom can make no mistakes. Mary and Martha did not think it was a good thing when God sent death, and took their brother away to the grave. It was grief and trial to them, and their hearts were ready to burst when they thought of that cold tomb and the silent, shrouded Lazarus sleeping the long sleep within it. But, after all, it was a good thing. Had their brother not died, they would not have seen the power of their Lord and Master so wonderfully displayed. Had not the sharp arrow of anguish entered their very soul, they would not have been drawn so near to Jesus, and have felt so precious the loving compassion of His great heart of love. Verily, the evil was a blessing in disguise.

And so it is with us all along our pilgrimage. The very things we think will do us harm are meant to do us good. In that night of toil and fear, when the disciples were out on the stormy sea struggling for very life, they saw a form treading upon the white-crested wave, and approaching them amid the dark gloom and raging wind, and they cried out with fear. They thought it was a spirit come to bid them to a watery grave; but, behold, it was the Lord Jesus Himself come to save and to rescue! Has this never been our experience? Have we not often thought we saw a spirit of woe when it was nought but the form of infinite love? Have we not often dreamed the end was near, when the next turn brought us face to face with salvation? Oh, be not faithless but believing! God will make all things work together for good to them that love Him! Sorrow and disappointment, and a rough road and a heavy cross, are hard to bear; but they bring us closer and closer to Him who has promised to give us rest. We might never have known the love of Christ if our hearts had been filled with the love of the world. We might never have known what a friend we had in God, had we not been forsaken by those of earth on whom we had set our affection. And God knows all this. And, with a loving Father's interest in us, He would give us just that which would tend to our good and withhold from us that which would be likely to give us evil. Happy are we if we submit ourselves to His blessed will!

But let us further apply this lesson of our text to our spiritual life. It is peculiarly in reference to matters of religion that we oftentimes feel something of unbelief in the Fatherhood of God. What is more common than meeting some one who is longing for an experience in spiritual things, that he never appears able to attain? There are some to whom God gives a deeper insight into His kingdom. They enjoy privileges which the ordinary Christian never seems to have. There was only one man in all the congregation of Israel with whom Jehovah spoke face to face, and that man was Moses. Among the disciples, it was only the beloved John that was permitted to lay his head upon the Saviour's bosom. These were men highly honoured among their fellows, and here and there, even now, we find some who, like Moses, are talking in the deep mysteries with the Lord, or like John, are peacefully resting upon His love, or like Mary, are sitting at His feet, listening to His words of joy and promise. But there are many in the fold who have not these rich blessings. There are many who are longing for them and praying for them, and yet they never come. And we, who are among these longing, praying ones, are very apt to wonder why God should give so much to one, and withhold a similar blessing from us. Why should God take one up into the Mount, and let another recline on His breast, and a third rest at His feet? And why should He withhold such

K

blessed privileges from so many others? It seems hard, very hard. We cannot tell why it is, but God knows. It may be were He to give us such good things, they would be too much for us. Our very blessings might make us proud. Even St. Paul, with all his grace, stood in danger of this very thing. He says, "Lest I should be exalted above measure through the abundance of the revelations, there was given to me a thorn in the flesh, the messenger of Satan to buffet me, lest I should be exalted above measure." And we may be very like the great Apostle. We may need some thorn in the flesh, lest we should be unduly lifted up. Nay, we may be such that it is better for God rather to hide than to reveal Himself—better to keep us in the darkness, than lead us at once out into the great and marvellous light. And though we may perhaps doubt this, for it is human nature to doubt, yet the doubt must surely vanish, when we remember the glorious assurance of our text. Can we not trust our heavenly Father to know how to give good gifts to His children? When it is a good thing for us to be as Moses, or John, or Mary, depend upon it God will give us that good thing. And as long as it is not a good thing for us, then let us beseech God not to give it us. Better for us not to see Him now, than, by seeing Him, to be lauded up with our privileges, and so run the risk of seeing Him no more for ever. Better to be without the rich and envied experience, than have that experience prove our ruin.

But perhaps the good thing that many of us would like to have, and which we have prayed for time and time again, is the consciousness of the personal forgiveness of sin, the consciousness that we are indeed reconciled to our heavenly Father. Yes, that consciousness is a good thing. It can make the soul very happy. It can fill the heart with a peace that passeth all understanding. But, for all that, God does not give it to every one. Many of us He requires to walk by faith, and not by sight. It is well it is so. We learn, then, not to put our trust in our feelings, but to throw ourselves entirely upon God's mercy. We feel that we are in such a helpless case, that we can only trust to God's love and power. And that is just the very place and condition I wish we were all in. I wish we were all brought to our wit's end, so that we would have no other way to turn than to God. It would make no difference then, about consciousness, or feeling, or experience—God may give it us or not, just as He sees fit—that is of small moment—but it is the promise "him that cometh unto Me I will in no wise cast out." Believe that, and though the consciousness is a good thing to have, yet if God withholds it, do not murmur, but submit to His gracious will. It may be a good thing for some to feel God, and in such cases our heavenly

Father knows how to give it, and He will give it. But there are many who will journey all the way to the better land, with nothing more than a trembling faith. They will have nothing but the promise to rest upon; nothing but the gracious invitation, "come," to urge them on. And, depend upon it, that is enough. We may be able to exclaim at the last, "Underneath are the everlasting arms," and we may feel them; or we may cry out, like good Christian, as he plunged into the dark river, "I sink in deep waters the billows go over my head, all his waves go over me." God may give us light, or He may give us darkness, and, in either case, they will be good. It was good for Christian to sink and to despond; it was good for Hopeful to be buoyed up and filled with joy.

I know there are some weary hearts that feel, because they have not the experiences some have, because they have not the deep-set consciousness of others, actually doubt whether they are really God's children. They fancy because God does not give them everything they think they ought to have, that He does not love them. It is hard for them to realize that God does not give them such things, because He knows they are better without them. They forget His Fatherhood. They forget His love and wisdom. They forget that, after all, they are but ignorant and wayward children. They cannot tell what is good or what evil. They make up their minds that they ought to have a certain thing, and because they thus want it, they call it good. But to them it may be anything but good, and so God keeps it from them. And because he does, this is no proof whatever that He has cast them off, or refused to care for them. On the contrary, it is one of the best of proofs that they are dear in His sight, and that He is watching for their safety. And whether He gives them a rich experience or not, it matters nothing.

There is a steamship entering the port. Its decks are crowded with eager-looking passengers. They see the lighthouse on the outer point, and the forts at the entrance, and the people on the pier. Oh, how beautiful everything looks, and how pleasant the smooth waters of the harbour after the rolling waves of the ocean, and how delightful the green trees and fields in the distance, after the long voyage across the trackless wilderness! They see it all, and rejoice. Their souls literally drink in the glorious prospect. But down in the cabin lies a sick man. He hears the exclamations of joy, and he longs to get up on deck. But he cannot. He is too ill to move. It would be almost certain death to him were he to gratify the longing desire. He must lie still, and see none of those beautiful sights. And there he lies, but the good ship goes on, and she gets to her appointed place, though he is left alone in his berth; and he, too, arrives in the quiet harbour, though he saw nothing of what his more favoured companions saw from the upper deck. And so there are many sailing heavenward in the Gospel ship, and some are on the upper deck and some are down below, but it makes no difference what they see, or where they are—they will all enter the port together. There will be the loving Johns and the doubting Thomases, there will be the bold, headstrong Peters, and the shrinking Nicodemuses, there will be the giants of great faith, and the last little babe that only peeped into the world and then left for the brighter home. They are all on board, and they will, every one of them, reach their Father's place at last!

It is not for us to question what God chooses to give us. If He sends us wealth and health, and joy and peace, we may be very thankful. But if he sees fit to send us poverty and sickness, and sorrow and adversity, oh, let us learn to trust Him! He knows just which of these two modes of treatment is best for us; oh, let us believe in His love! We do not know which of them is good for us. There is but one thing that we know beyond a doubt is of the highest value—that we know is without the shadow of evil. And that one thing is the one thing needful, the salvation of the Lord Jesus Christ! Have we that priceless treasure? Is it now the joy of our hearts, the strength of our soul? Do we want it? Oh, what a solemn question! Do we want Jesus as our own—our own dear Saviour,

our own loving Master, our own elder Brother? Then ask for Him. He is worth more than all the other good things put together—either those of this world or the next—yea, more than all, were they ten thousand times as many! The vast universe of God has no gift that may with Him compare!

But perhaps we think He is only for the children, and it may be we feel that we are not children of God. We may be among those who cannot realize the Fatherhood of God. And, therefore, we feel that Jesus may not be ours—that none of the good things of God may be ours. But thanks be to God, the text settles that point once and for all! It does not say that God will give good things to His children, but that He will give good things to them that ask Him!—*to them that ask Him!* Oh, what a broad promise! Whether we know that we are His children or not—no matter how full we may be of doubts on that point—it is simply to them that ask Him! The wandering prodigal, the sin-stained sinner, the forlorn outcast, may receive every good thing of God, if they will but ask Him. Mercy and grace and salvation may be ours—the Lord Jesus Christ may be ours—if we will but ask. "Ask and ye shall receive." Oh, what loving words! Oh, what a message to the soul hungering and thirsting after righteousness! God is indeed our Father; but lest we should doubt, He says He will give good things to them that ask Him! Are we among the askers?

Are we among those who are asking for the Pearl of great price—for God's greatest and best gift to man? Never mind anything else! Let us not be disappointed if we get nothing else! With Jesus we have all we need! He *is* all, and if God gives us nothing but Him, we are rich indeed! Oh, ask for Him, and leave the rest with God! "For if ye, being evil, know how to give good gifts unto your children, how much more shall your Father which is in heaven give good things to them that ask Him?"

May God bless these words, so that they may rest in the heart of every one who reads them; for the Redeemer's sake. Amen.

SERMON XIII.

THE BLESSINGS OF FAITH.

ROMANS XV. 13 :—"Now the God of hope fill you with all joy and peace in believing, that ye may abound in hope through the power of the Holy Ghost."

SOME would tell us that there is nothing in Christian faith—that it is only a superstition—a legacy of the ignorance of unenlightened times. They would destroy that faith, and show us how unreasonable it is, and how degrading to man to hold it. But the fact meets such here that men are sinners, and he who has a keen consciousness of sin, and is convinced that sin has its own reward, will naturally seek some way of escape. The same law that will induce the sick man to go to the physician will compel the sinner to seek some remedy for the disease that is destroying his very soul. And what remedy shall he take? Experience tells us that the world has no remedy. Experience tells us that science and advanced thought cannot heal a sin-sick soul. And experience further tells us that we cannot cure ourselves. No; but Christianity says, "Believe on the Lord Jesus Christ and thou shalt be saved." This is the remedy that the Word of God proposes. It has been tried, and never known to fail. It is the only thing in heaven or in earth that can meet the want of the awakened sinner, or that can satisfy the longings of the contrite heart. I shall endeavour to show how true this is. I shall show that there is something in Christian faith—that it is not an idle superstition—or anything less than a gift from above to poor fallen man.

As a proof of this, our text states that there is joy, and peace, and hope, in believing. At the same time, we are reminded that these blessings come from God, and that they abound in us through the power of the Holy Ghost. We must, therefore, never forget to give God the glory. He gives us faith, and with the faith He gives us joy, and peace, and hope.

Let us, then, in the *first* place, look at the JOY THERE IS IN BELIEVING.

The religion of the Lord Jesus is peculiarly a religion of joy. We are commanded to "rejoice evermore." "Rejoice in the Lord alway," says St. Paul, "and again I say, Rejoice." "Let thy saints," exclaims David, "shout for joy." There is no room for sadness in faith. We may be, as the apostle said, "sorrowful," and yet should we always rejoice.

There are, it is true, times when the spirit is bowed down with anguish, yet even then there is a bright side to the dark cloud. We have One to whom we can unburden our sorrows. We have One in whom we can confide, on whom we can rest. We have one who will sympathize with us, and go with us into the darkness of tribulation, into the valley of the shadow of death. The very consciousness that we have such a Friend as this is enough to make our hearts rejoice! There are times, too, when temptation is almost irresistible. Sin stands before us in most alluring form, appealing to our strongest passion. We are, as the poor bird under the fascinating power of the serpent, unable to escape. We know the danger—we know that death lurks beneath those poisonous fangs. Oh, that we might ever hear in that awful moment the words of the Apostle, "Believe —believe on the Lord Jesus Christ and thou shalt be saved!" He has power to save us from temptation. He can pluck us out of the mouth of the serpent of sin. He can impart almighty strength to us in the moment of weakness. The faith that can lay hold of this glorious truth must fill us with joy and gladness. In temptation and in sorrow He can save. "When thou passest through the waters I will be with thee; and through the rivers they shall not overflow thee: when thou walkest through the fire, thou shalt not be burned; neither shall the flame kindle upon thee." There is unspeakable joy in believing that blessed promise.

And who can deny the joy that thrills the soul of the repentant sinner when by faith he beholds Christ as his Saviour? He sees the sin. It drags him to the dust. It paralyzes his very spirit with anguish and woe. There is death before him. The billows of the sea of wrath are roaring for their prey. An eternity of misery dawns upon him. The sure vengeance of an offended God prepares to break upon him. Then comes the cry—louder than the storm's wild thunder—"What must I do to be saved?" It pierces the clouds of condemnation—it reaches heaven's high throne—it brings its own reply: "I am with thee to save thee, and to deliver thee, saith the Lord." And what says the poor sinner? "Lord, I believe, help Thou mine unbelief." Is there not joy in that faith? A brand plucked from the burning—a sinner saved from the jaws of eternal death—a whole life of iniquity blotted out by an act of grace—no joy, no gladness in believing this? Ask those who have this faith. Ask those who have been alone with Jesus at the foot of the Cross. Ask those who on the verge of death's cold flood, are yet full of joy, ready to burst into songs of praise at the glorious prospect before them. Whence their joy? Whence the joy that makes glad the Christian, wherever he may be, in life or in death? Most certainly in nothing else than in the faith he has in his Lord and Master. What is sin to him—what cares he whether there be a hell—what is death? He believes in the Lord Jesus Christ, and whosoever believes in Him shall be saved. That is enough. The sinner may well be glad.

There is in Europe an order of Monks, the rules of which denounce mirth and joy. The members of of that community are immured for life in dark, gloomy cloisters. They observe perpetual silence.

No smile is allowed to play upon their sad, sad features. They think it a sin to laugh or to be happy. They think it the height of Christian perfection to be gloomy and silent. But they cannot know what true faith is. Believing on the Lord does not produce this effect on men. When the poor jailer was converted, we are told that he brought Paul and Silas into his house and " set meat before them and rejoiced, believing in God with all his house." He had heard that which was indeed good news. And what it did for him it does for all. It makes them happy. They want no gloomy cell, with its sad, perpetual silence. It is not night with them, but cheerful, happy day. It is life now and bright sunshine. " They break forth into singing." They have but one thought : " I will be glad and rejoice in Thy mercy."

Such is Christian faith. What is there to give a poor, weary, heavy-laden sinner better than that ? What can be given him that will make him as happy ? Here is a something that can and does answer the longings of his heart. It removes the load of sin. It takes away the fear of retribution. It links him with God. In sin, in temptation, in sorrow, there is a Saviour, One mighty to save. He believes in Him, he rests on Him, he is saved by Him. There is no uncertain present, no dark future. It is full, loving, sure salvation. Believe that, and we must be glad. A trial of it will settle every doubt. Untold multitudes have tried it, and are now rejoicing in the Lord. They praise Him now; hereafter they shall praise Him with a new and glorious song. Depend upon it there is joy in believing.

But, in the *second* place, our text tells us that there is PEACE IN BELIEVING.

There can be no peace in the heart of the sinner until he is sure of forgiveness from God. Estranged from God, no man can be happy. He must be distracted with fears. " Thou hidest Thy face," says the Psalmist, " they are troubled." When a traveller is in a dangerous and unknown wild, enveloped in the darkness of midnight, he will very naturally be troubled. He can see no way, he knows no way, by which to reach the haven of safety. He gets bewildered, distracting thoughts possess him, he is in despair. Such is the sinner who is conscious of having lost his way in the dark night of this world's sin. He is troubled. He cannot be otherwise. He is alone, exposed to great dangers, nay, in peril of eternal death. He knows of no way of escape. True, there may be others with him, but they are in a like condition. They are all lost together. And though each one has a plan to propose, it does no good. But when the good Shepherd comes, and takes up in his arms that which was lost, then the trouble vanishes. The child has no fear when with its father, be the night never so dark, the way never so rough. The father knows the way. That is enough. So God knows the dangers of the wilderness, and when we can trust Him, believing that He has power to save, then are we at peace. All the doubts, the anguish, the despair are at an end. We have peace in believing.

We can judge of the truth of this by our own experience, and by observation. St. Paul tells us that "God hath called us to peace." We may not be able in words to express that peace—it is a peace which passeth all understanding—but surely when we know that God has put away our sin, that He has blotted out our iniquity, that He has reconciled us unto Himself—surely, then, I say, a feeling of peaceful security must be ours. Any one who has grace enough to realize the perilous condition of the sinner, must feel troubled and distressed at the thought of his sad end; but remove everything, and give him a free title to heaven, and he has no further cause for fear. Have we believed and not realized this peace? Have we not seen it in others whom we know are followers of the Lord? There are people who are distressed by the want of this world's goods, and there are people who are distressed with the abundance of them; but if they have faith in Christ, they are at peace in their poverty, and at peace in their wealth. The soldier, if he believe in God, has peace though on the field of battle. In the most trying circumstances of life, if we are one with God, there is peace. We are given rich foretastes of that future peace which shall be ours through all eternity. Oh, that we might realize this now in fuller measure!

> "O for the peace which floweth as a river,
> Making life's desert places bloom and smile!
> O for the faith to grasp heaven's bright forever,
> Amid the shadows of earth's little while!"

Depend upon it, if we have not more peace with our faith, it is not faith's fault. Our faith is not altogether right. The prisoner who holds in his hand his Sovereign's free pardon is not distressed at the Judge's sentence. Neither, though the law condemn us, need we fear when we have God's forgiveness, written in the letters of our Saviour's blood. Having that forgiveness, we should be at peace. We know we have it by faith. We take hold of it by faith. The prisoner did not hear the king pronounce his pardon, but he believes it none the less. It is written in black and white. So is our pardon on the pages of God's blessed book. A free and absolute release! Is there not peace in believing that? What else in all the wide, wide world will bring true peace to the contrite sinner's soul? Is there anything? Where is it? Thousands and tens of thousands have searched for it, and are still searching for it, but they have never found it, and will never find it anywhere else than in a living faith in Christ Jesus. Faith in Him will bring peace—peace now, eternal peace hereafter. Oh, if we are in trouble, then let us believe Him—let us trust

Him—let us take Him at His word! He will save —save unto the uttermost—only believe! Then shall we find rest in the Lord, then shall we in our own experience prove that there is indeed peace in believing.

But, in the *third* place, there is HOPE IN BELIEVING—and that the best and surest of hope.

It is not all present gain—there is a future full of promise and glory, and it is man's future that is of far more importance than his present. The question of what that future shall be is full of consequence to every one. Shall it be an eternity of happiness, or an eternity of misery? Shall we be forever with the Lord, or forever banished from His presence? No one can lightly regard such questions as these. Nor can any one wilfully go on to misery. But how escape it? How win happiness and heaven? The world proposes many ways, but what is there in them? Men try them, but in the end they find there is no hope. They build upon them, but find they are sinking sand. How different with true religion! "Believe on the Lord Jesus Christ and thou shalt be saved." Have faith in Him, and there is hope. What can give such hope as that? The God whom we have offended declares forgiveness. The God who holds our destiny in His hands has pledged Himself to give us eternal happiness. The future is safe, because He has made it so. His word is sure. It gives us hope. We have nothing to fear. Sins forgiven, an atonement wrought, a rest provided, we have everything we need. Nor ought we to doubt. "I know," says St. Paul, " whom I have believed, and am persuaded that He is able to keep that which I have committed to Him against that day." We have committed to Him our souls. We throw ourselves absolutely upon His mercy. We look to Him for salvation. We believe He will save. We therefore hope in Him. He is the Hope of Israel—the Hope of all His believing people. There can be no real, substantial hope save in Him.

> "Our hope is built on nothing less,
> Than Jesus' blood and righteousness."

But what a glorious hope that is? No change in it! No disappointment! God cannot lie. He can neither deceive our faith nor wither our hope. Earthly hopes may be false. But this hope never. It rests upon the word of the Almighty God—it is built upon the everlasting Rock of the eternal ages! Men may scoff and sceptics may sneer—but this hope has withstood the assaults of many generations, the fires of martyrdom, the war of a raging hell. It has cheered and will still cheer man in his weakness, and man in his distress. He whose life is full of it knows no night. He whose life is full of it has the early golden rays of the heavenly day cast across the path of his pilgrimage, and already hears in the still eventide the far-off song of the Redeemed, the murmur of the many waters, in the Paradise of God. What is it that cheers the life and brightens the death of God's people? What is it that kills sorrow and banishes distress? What is it that brings heaven down to earth, and takes earth up to heaven? Simply faith—faith in God—faith in His promises, in His love, in His power. Nothing but faith. Any other hope is not to be depended upon. But faith in God brings hope with it. The better the faith, the better the hope. "Faith is the substance of things hoped for." If we believe, then, we know that "our Lord Jesus Christ himself and God, even our Father, hath loved us, and hath given us everlasting consolation and good hope through grace." We have hope in believing. We may look forward to a glorious future. We may rest sure that all will be well. We may leave everything with Him.

We have then in Faith, Joy, Peace and Hope. Has not faith, then, its blessings? Is it an empty superstition? The general characteristic of superstition is fear—not joy. There is neither joy, peace, nor hope in superstition. But Christian faith has all three qualities in fullest measure. Nor is this faith the result of ignorance, for the more able we are intelligently to ascertain the ground of it the greater and stronger it will become. The saving element of faith may, indeed, be grasped by those of small intellectual ability, but as they grow in knowledge they will behold the things of God in a broader, grander light, and their joy will be deeper, their peace more sincere, their hope more confident. Of one thing we may be very certain, that faith can do that for man which nothing else can do. We see people trying to solve difficult questions—one man comes out with a pretty theory apparently very reasonable, and another man sends forth a theory just as pretty and apparently just as reasonable, but absolutely contradictory, and if a third individual is not found to contradict the both, it will be very strange. Now, suppose one's soul is at stake on a question of this kind—and many of our souls are at stake,—what shall we do? One says do this and all will be well, and another says do something else. We feel that we must believe something—those very individuals that run down Christian faith, after all, do believe something—man must believe something —what shall it be? Shall it rest upon what men say, or upon what God says? Perhaps some may say they do not believe there is a God. But which is easier, to believe there is no God, or to believe there is a God? There is faith in either case. But what is there in the faith of the man who believes in no God? Nothing. And what is there in the faith of that which rests upon man's sayings, and man's reasonings? Nothing but uncertainty and gloom. Believe in God and there is joy, and peace, and hope. Deny it those who can. Let us try it for ourselves, and we shall find how true is the Apostle's assertion.

One thing is certain, we have all a soul to save. If the devil can laugh us out of saving it, he will. If the world can keep us in sin and misery, it will. Let us open our eyes to our danger! See death standing in our pathway. Know that destruction awaits us at our journey's end. O dear reader, listen not to the syren's song. Hearken not to the rippling music of the waters of the sea of woe, that now, perhaps, is lulling you to sleep, but would, had it the power, sing the loud, sad requiem over your eternal misery. Up, up, turn to God. Believe, believe on the Lord Jesus Christ while you have yet time—and you shall be saved. Settle this question now once and for all. Do not pass it by. Think over it. Pray over it. Talk over it. Only have faith, and your soul will rejoice and be glad in the Lord,—you will find peace and rest now, and you will have a sure and perfect hope for the future. May God help you to do this—may He give you of His grace that you may take these truths home to yourself—and may "the God of hope fill you with all joy and peace in believing, that ye may abound in hope through the power of the Holy Ghost."

SERMON XIV.

THE GUIDANCE OF GOD.

Psalm xxxvii. 23.—" The steps of a good man are ordered by the Lord."

ALL people have not the same faith. In one person faith is strong, in another it is weak. Nay, in the same individual it changes: to-day it is firm and unwavering, to-morrow it is doubtful and questioning. Perhaps in nothing more do we perceive these degrees of faith than in ourselves or in others when the Providence of God is concerned. One man sees the hand of God in everything he does, no matter how small it may be. Another only sees God in the great affairs of life. The Psalmist was one who firmly believed that God overruled everything that concerned His people. Even "the steps"—the daily life—the little things —"of a good man are ordered by the Lord." He has laid out the way in which we are to go—He leads us in that way—He guides us unto the end. If our faith were only strong enough to take in this blessed truth, it would remove much of the burden of care and anxiety that oftentimes rests upon us. Surely we have all need to pray, " Lord, increase our faith." Let us then see how true is the statement of our text—how easily it may be shown that God does indeed direct the way of His people.

"The steps of a good man are ordered by the Lord." This is proved, in the *first place*, by the fact that GOD RULES ALL THINGS, BOTH GREAT AND SMALL.

He is the sovereign Ruler of the universe. He is the Lord of all. Nothing is exempt from His authority. The bright worlds that wend their way amid the depths of the unfathomable space move only at His bidding, and in accordance with His laws. The sun casts its glory across the silent solitude, and touches planet, moon, and star with golden light at His command. The blazing comet beats with fiery speed along a path laid out by the Great Creator through the trackless heavens. We know that some power must rule those bodies, vast and mighty though they be. We know, too, that some power rules this earth on which we live. Day and night, summer and winter, seed time and harvest, come with too great regularity to admit of chance. The waters of the boundless ocean, we are told, are in the hollow of his hand. He sends forth the storm that crowns the wild billows with snow-white foam. At His command the winds cease, the raging sea is stilled. He is Lord of that mighty wilderness. So is He Governor among the nations. He raises up a people to great glory and honour: again He scatters the inhabitants of the earth. He makes a land to flow with milk and honey: again He lays it bare, and brands it with desolation. In all the great things of the world and of the universe we see the finger of God. They come into existence, they move and fulfil their office at His bidding. Surely it is hard to doubt that which is plain to everyone who cares to see it.

And if God thus controls the great things, have we not a reason for maintaining that He also controls the little things? There is a little rill trickling down the mountain side. It is but a thin silver thread amid the green mossy rocks. But, as it dashes along, other little rills join their little streams with it, and it grows bigger and bigger till it reaches the valley and becomes a brook. And brooks flowing into each other make rivers. And the river broadens and grows deeper as it pours along towards the sea, and joins its waters with the waters of many other rivers that fill the great ocean bed. God's law reaches those little mountain rills so that they all struggle to reach the sea. And behold another evidence of His power, though they are forever adding to the sea, yet the sea never overflows its appointed bounds. And why? Because yon bright sun is drawing up those ocean waters in small minute drops, and these drops are gathered into clouds, and the winds waft them back over the land, and they are discharged in refreshing showers and fertilizing rains. Mountain rills are small things, and drops of vapour are smaller still, and yet they are under laws as truly made by God as are the laws that control the boundless space. Nor could God rule the greater things of His kingdom without ruling the lesser things. The great ones are made up of little ones. The ocean is but a vast mass of little globules. Even the earth itself is but a conglomeration of atoms, and great as it seems to be to us, it is, when compared with the mighty universe, both small and insignificant. If the little things were not controlled so as to be combined into great things there could be no great things, and consequently, where we now see perfect order and marvellous grandeur, all would be anarchy and confusion.

The same guiding power is evident in the animal world. Its teeming wonders abundantly proclaim the one great truth. All are in God's mind. The giant elephant roaming amid Indian forests is not more the object of His care than the fragile humming bird that darts about our gardens, or the short-lived gnat that plays in the evening shade beneath the river willows, or the minute animalcule whose tiny world lies hid within a little drop of water. These are all accomplishing the work laid out for them by God. They move as regularly within their sphere as the hosts of heaven move in the mysterious orbits made for them by the Almighty Creator. And when we think of this surely we cannot doubt that God rules all things, both great and small.

If, then, we find this true in everything we see around us, have we not good reason for supposing that man comes under the same rule? Shall all the universe be controlled by God and man be exempt? True, we have rebelled against God—the only one of all His works that has denied His authority—but there are those who have returned to their allegiance, and would serve Him, and it is of these I speak. They are obedient, shall they, then, not be led by God? Shall He not guide them in all the affairs of life—even the smallest? He guides the little rill to the ocean, shall He not guide them to the ocean of His love? He takes up the little mist-drop from the watery-wilderness and bears it on the wings of the wind to the thirsty land, shall He not also take them up in His arms and bear them to the home of His presence—to a home where they are needed—to a presence thirsting with very love for their souls? I feel that in this fact that God overrules everything, we have a good reason for believing that "the steps of a good man are ordered by the Lord." I cannot see why we should be excepted from the rule.

But, in the *second* place, we find a reason in GOD'S PURPOSES CONCERNING MAN.

God did not create man for nought. He had a purpose in his creation. Nor did He create him for this life only. There is an existence beyond the present. We believe that this is a probationary time—a time of preparation. We are to be fitted for a higher, a more glorious, an eternal life. God has made us to inherit His kingdom—to reign with Him as princes in a world of joy and peace. If this is God's purpose, then it must of necessity be that God Himself is preparing us for that destiny. No one else could do it, for no one else knows what the future will be. So we are called upon to undergo pain and suffering, and to endure temptation and tribulation. We must be brought to a knowledge of the truth, and be led in the way of life. This is all the work of God. Just as materials are prepared specifically for a building, so are we made ready for a certain position in God's great temple. Some of us will occupy one station, some another. None but God knows what will be the work and office of each individual of the Redeemed in that blessed land; and none but God knows even what our work is in this life. He has purposes for every one of us. There is a rich man. His heart is buried in his wealth. He neither knows nor fears God. But one day he finds his riches are all gone. He is a poor man. And then he thinks of religion. He turns to God. He finds that which passes all understanding—all earthly wealth. God's purpose was to take that man unto Himself, but so long as his heart clung to the things of this world it was impossible, and so the blow was struck, and the stricken soul found refuge in the Rock of Ages.

In one of the convents of Germany, some three hundred and seventy years ago, was an old, pious, God-fearing monk. He had spent his days unknown and unnoticed in the gloomy life of the cloister. No doubt he often thought how useless he had been. He had done no great work to leave as a memorial in the world's history. Indeed, he lived only for the Master's glory. In the same convent was a young man of wonderful mental powers, humility, and devotion. He was earnestly striving to live the new life. His soul yearned after God. But he saw no light. He was in deep despair. One day the old man met him and asked him why he looked so sad? "Because," answered the young monk, "I do not know what will become of me. It is no use for me to make promises to God—sin is ever the strongest." With great simplicity, and from the fulness of his heart, the aged monk reminded him of the article of the Creed, "I believe in the forgiveness of sin," and he expounded it in such a way as to show that God freely forgave His poor erring children, and only asked them to trust Him. "Oh, my friend," he said, "instead of torturing yourself on account of your sins cast yourself by faith into the Redeemer's arms—look at the wounds of Jesus Christ—to the blood that he has shed for you." His words sank deep into the young man's heart. The cloud passed away from his face. His soul was filled with joy. The old man's work on earth was done. But the doctrine that he had given that young man was the doctrine that ere long flashed in living power and glory throughout Europe, and showed to sinning man the way of salvation through the Redeeming Lord. God had a purpose for that aged monk. He gave him to drink of the waters of life. He led him to the cross. And then he gave the truth to Martin Luther—and with that truth Martin Luther shook the world. Surely the steps of a good man are ordered by the Lord.

It is very true that we cannot understand God's dealings with us. They seem so different from what we would expect. "What I do thou knowest not now; but thou shalt know hereafter." When we reach the other shore we shall see the purpose God had for us in this life, and the purpose He has for us in that better life. If we cannot see it now we shall see it then that He was our guide in all things. It seems plain even now. God leads His people to the Saviour. They do not go themselves. He leads them through life. By what numberless little things we can trace His hand in all we do. There is a purpose in them all. The sick-bed has its purpose. The heavy Cross has its purpose. The cloud of sorrow has its purpose. We must be made meet for the Master's kingdom—whether it be in this world or in the world to come. We cannot fit ourselves. The old monk in the convent of Erfurt could not have worked a reformation in Europe.

He knew nothing of what was coming. But God did, and God alone could prepare the way for it. He guided the whole thing. And so with us individually—whatever God's determination concerning us may be, He will bring it to pass. He will, by little and little lead us along, and His purpose in the end will be accomplished. He directs the way of His people.

We see the truth of this, in the *third* place, in GOD'S LOVE FOR HIS PEOPLE.

God's love for His people is compared to that of a father's for his children. It is said to be even greater and stronger. We may, then, gather something of how God works from the way earthly parents work with their offspring. They are given to them to train up in the fear and admonition of the Lord. From infancy the body and the mind are watched and tended. Step by step the child is led along through the years of its youth till it can care for itself. It is warned of this error, and taught the sin of that, and drawn to that which is good. Were it left to itself, it would die, or come to an evil end. But the father's love cares for it and guides it. So our heavenly Father's love cares for us and guides us all the days of our life.

It would be contrary to God's nature to do otherwise. We cannot conceive of an earthly father having a great love for his child and neglecting it. The world would justly say his love was false.

Would it not be so with God? Love prompts us to action. It prompted Him so that He gave His only-begotten Son for our salvation. Does it not lead Him further to care for us individually? A little helpless child does not need its mother's care and guidance more than we need God's. We do not know what our next step may be. The action we are about to take may be for good or for evil—who knows? Yet God says to His people "there shall no evil befall thee." God's love would not permit it to happen to us. Then He must guide us into that which is for our good. He must lead us in the way His love has marked out for us. If no evil shall befall us, then it can only be because God will keep us from it.

Then, again, God's love has prepared for us a heaven of rest. But unless God teaches us the way there we shall never enter in. We need to be led step by step, and this is what God does. The love He has for His people would never stop at providing a home for them when they could not of themselves reach it, but it would go out to them, and find the lost and guide the blind. The many examples we have of the way God exercises His love prove how true this is. There was Paul. He was trained in the arts and sciences at Tarsus. Then he was led to Jerusalem, and, under the care of one of the greatest masters of the day, he became well versed in the law and traditions of his fathers. He was devoted to the old religion. But God turned his wonderful talents in an opposite direction. He became the great champion of Christianity. He advocated its cause in Athens, Rome and Corinth, and throughout the great empire. Thousands were converted under his ministry in his own day—untold thousands have been converted and strengthened by his writings since. His will be an honoured name on the lips of every child of God throughout eternity. Why was he so manifestly guided in everything he did? Because the Lord loved His people, and He raised them up a great apostle to show them the living way. His love led him to care for them. His love led Him to prepare a faithful minister to guide them. There are many instances such as this—in fact, they abound unnumbered and meet us everywhere. They confirm the words of Jehovah: "I have loved thee with an everlasting love." And in the fact of that love we know that "the steps of a good man are ordered by the Lord." He directs the way of His people.

These are three reasons proving the truth of our text. We know that God rules all things, both great and small. We know that He has gracious purposes concerning His people. We know that He has great love. And, therefore, we cannot but conclude that He is our guide in everything we do. Shall we not, then, trust Him? Shall not our faith become stronger? Shall we not depend upon Him in the little things as well as in the great ones? That was a beautiful lesson Luther learned when looking out of his window one summer evening. He saw on a tree a little bird making its arrangements for a night's rest. "Look," said he, "how that little fellow preaches faith to us all. He takes hold of his twig, tucks his head under his wing and goes to sleep, *leaving God to think for him.*" "Ye are of more value," said Jesus, "than many sparrows." Oh, that we could in all we say and do leave God to think for us! We should come out all right in the end then. We should see that God knows what is best, and does indeed work all things together for good to them that love Him. "The steps of a good man are ordered by the Lord."

This is a lesson which we need to learn— a truth we need to take home to ourselves. Depend upon it, life would be far happier could we only believe that the Lord was leading us. I know how hard it is to do so. Some of us are doubtful and hesitating all our life long. We shall, perhaps, carry our doubts with us to the grave. Bunyan's "Christian" was full of despair when he was crossing the dark river that separated him from the celestial city. He could not see that the Lord was leading him through the deep waters. "He had horror of mind and heart-fears that he should die in that river, and never obtain entrance in at the gate.' With "Hopeful" it was very different. He could cry out to his brother pilgrim, "I feel the bottom and it is good." No doubt many and many a true child of God will go through life and through death with but a weak and wavering faith in God's providence, while others will trust Him through all, and exclaim at the very last, as a dear brother did not long ago, "I am sweeping through the gates, washed in the blood of the Lamb." There will be doubting Thomases and loving, trusting Johns as long as there is a saint left on earth. But, oh, if we could only cast aside these clinging doubts—if we could only be as little children—if we could but believe that He who guides the stars in empty space and rules over all the works of His hand guides us also—would not life be brighter and we happier? Let us, then, remember the purposes and the love of God, and cast all our cares upon Him. Let us by faith take hold of His hand and go with Him, step by step, in the way He is leading us. It may be all dark around, with no light ahead—has it not, my Christian reader, seemed so with you in many a trying circumstance? Has not your future been buried beneath dark heavy clouds?—But if it is in God's way, can you not leave it with Him and trust Him with your all? I believe that these doubts arise from too much looking at self and not enough to God. We sometimes forget that He is everything, we are nothing. If we kept this ever before us—if we would ever look to Him as the little tender plant looks to the sun for its growth and colour and strength, or as the little child looks to its earthly parent for food and love and guidance—our faith would grow stronger as we grow older—we should see the hand of God in all the affairs of life, both great and small.

There is, however, this comfort to the Christian seeking to serve his Master—that weak though the faith may be—trembling as may be the trust—God does lead him, God does guide him, God does lay out his way for him. So that we shall be led to our home, we shall be guided to our rest, God's purposes concerning us will be fulfilled! Thank God for this! Thank God He deals with us not so much as we deserve, but in accordance with His love! Thanks be to God "the steps of a good man are ordered by the Lord!"

May our earnest prayer to our Father in heaven be, "For Thy name's sake lead me and guide me," and may we realize the glorious truth that He does lead us in the paths of righteousness, and will so lead us unto our life's end!

SERMON XV.

THE LAST REST.

Hebrews iv. 9:—"There remaineth therefore a rest to the people of God."

ST. PAUL is writing to the Hebrews—to God's ancient people—of things which were then present. Among other matters, he is showing them that the Sabbath rest, which had been repeatedly promised to their forefathers, had never been realized under the old dispensation. The rest of Canaan was not all. There was more for Israel than that. And, therefore, he argues, if God has promised a rest, and that rest has not been attained, "There remaineth a rest to the people of God,"—a rest yet to come. This rest, he says, is to be found in the Gospel dispensation—in the new order of things brought about by the coming of the Lord Jesus Christ. It does not need much to show the truth of this doctrine. The old law knew nothing of a Saviour, or of the peace which that Saviour could give. It was a religion of works. There was an unrest, an uncertainty, a gloom about it, in part occasioned by its being only a dim foreshadowing of things that were yet to come. In the Gospel, all this had passed away. In the new dispensation, all was light. The sinner saw plainly the way of salvation. He might have peace and joy. He need no longer be troubled with the fulfilment of duties which he was unable to perform. He might rest in a Saviour's love and mercy.

Yet, doubtless, even this more perfect rest, is but a better and richer foretaste of the rest which remaineth for the people of God, in the blessed home beyond the grave. It is to this rest that we are yet looking; "For here we have no continuing city, but we seek one to come." Though we have a more perfect rest than had the Jew of old, yet our longings for the fuller rest are not satisfied. We are still in the wilderness, travelling homeward. This life is often compared to a pilgrimage. We are ever journeying on through sickness, temptation, and sorrow. Trials of all sorts beset us on the way. Enemies stand in our path. And it is oftentimes a hard battle we are called upon to fight, a heavy cross we are called upon to bear, a dark night we are called upon to travel in. And, such being the case, we long for rest. We long for the time to come, when these temptations and trials shall have an end, when the eternal day shall open upon us with all its glories, when we shall sit down and rest beside the still waters of Paradise. It is the hope of that rest that cheers us now in many a painful, trying hour. It is the promise of that rest that irradiates the gloom of many a sad, sad life. It is the certainty of that rest that spurs us on to renewed exertion, to more earnest toil. Truly, besides the rest promised us under the Gospel, we may apply our text also to the rest in yon world of peace. Hath not God said, " There remaineth yet a rest for His people ? "

What are some of the prominent features of that rest ?

In the *first* place, it is A FUTURE REST. We have not yet reached it. To be sure, we have more premonitions of it, a richer and better conception of it, than had the Jew of old. Like the beloved disciple, we may lean upon our Saviour's bosom, and find rest there. We may lay our burden of sin at the foot of the Cross. We may throw off the bondage of Satan, and take upon us the light and easy yoke of Christ. We may leave the doubts and fears of the law, and rejoice in the full liberty of the Gospel. In all this we may enjoy much rest. But we have still much work to do. We have still a great adversary to contend with, strong temptations to resist, besetting sins to avoid. We have still, in our weakness, a God to glorify, a God to obey, a God to love. There are sorrows to be borne, and virtues to be practised, and fellow sinners to be saved. So that we have not yet entered into perfect rest. This is a fact we must ever bear in mind. We have not yet reached home. This world is not our home. Prosperity in this life is not the crown of glory which God has promised to His faithful ones. He does not always give us peace and joy in this world.

Oftentimes He fills up for us a cup of bitterest gall. A heavy cross is prepared for us to bear. A dark cloud is cast over all our hopes. Instead of giving us those things in which our souls delight, He sends us bereavement, and affliction, and persecution. Instead of surrounding us with the sweet quiet of the heavenly calm, the rushing tempest and the wild storm await us. We are tossed to and fro upon life's unknown ocean, in distress and in danger, in perplexities and in fears.

But, oh! how sweet to think that, after all this is over, there is yet a rest to the people of God! The broken wreck of a vessel, almost ruined by the furious waves, shall yet reach the haven of peace and safety. The weary pilgrim who, with tired step and trembling heart, has persevered in the heavenward journey, will enter the gate of the celestial city by and bye. The returning prodigal will sit down in his father's house at last. There will be an end—a happy end—to all these sufferings. The cross shall be transformed into the crown; sorrow into joy; the storm into calm; the dark night into the bright and ever-glorious day. We shall enter into rest.

There is in this much that should cheer us in our work and in our sorrow. We shall not always be toiling—not always under the rod. There will be peace and joy at the last. There will be a lifting up of the cloud. We should not murmur, then, at

God's mysterious dispensations. We should not seek to get rid of the cross—whatever that cross may be which we are called upon to bear. We should not try to avoid the work which we are given to do. We must expect that in this world we shall have tribulation. The Master was a man of sorrows and acquainted with grief, He had no place to lay His head, He was despised and scorned of men. And shall we be greater than our Lord? Shall we go through life without the thorny crown, the toil, the grief? No; we cannot expect that. The way to heaven is a narrow way—a way in which there is great danger, many enemies, many temptations. We have to persevere in that way unto the end. Nor can we enter into glory unless we have persevered. We cannot rest unless we have worked. We cannot wear the laurels unless we have fought the battle.

And seeing that the rest is future, we ought not to expect rest in the time present. Now is the time for work. We are put into this world for labour. Talents are given us and grace is bestowed upon us that we should do God good service. We have to use those talents and show ourselves worthy of that grace. We are not to sit down and rest and say this world is heaven. Nor are we to rest in our present spiritual attainments, but to grow in grace —to go on and on to perfection. Every day that we follow Christ we grow stronger, and are capable of more work, and we have to do that work.

And let no one say he has no work to do. As long as he has a friend or a neighbour unconverted, as long as he has himself an evil temper to conquer, or an indolent state of soul to amend, or things to learn of God and religion, he has work to do. It may be very hard sometimes to do this work. But it must be work now, rest by and bye. Grief and temptation and persecution must be borne now, the glory will be hereafter. Let us remember this. The rest that remaineth for the people of God is a future rest. It is in our Father's home—in the many mansions which the Saviour has gone to prepare for those who love Him. Nor should we consider the trials we have to go through in this life too severe or too bitter. They have their end. "For our light affliction, which is but for a moment, worketh for us a far more exceeding and eternal weight of glory." "We must, through much tribulation, enter into the kingdom of God." And after all, "the sufferings of this present time are not worthy to be compared with the glory which shall be revealed in us." We shall know by and bye the secret of much that is now so mysterious to us. The heavier we have toiled, the sweeter shall be our rest. The darker the night, the brighter the day. The more lowly the cross, the more exalted the crown. The nearer to the Master in suffering, the nearer to the Master in glory. All this will be evident in the great hereafter. Then let us comfort ourselves with this blessed hope. Let us rejoice in tribulation. Let us look away from the things of earth to the things of heaven. Let us watch for our Lord's coming, " bearing all things, believing all things, hoping all things, enduring all things." And, moreover, "beloved, seeing that ye look for such things, be diligent that ye may be found of Him in peace, without spot, and blameless." " Set your affections on things above, not on things on the earth." For we have not yet entered into rest; " there remaineth, therefore, a rest to the people of God." May God bring us to that rest! May He comfort us with sweet and strengthening foretastes of it! May He guide us through the wilderness to the home of His presence!

> " Oh, spread thy covering wings abroad
> Till all our wanderings cease,
> And at our Father's loved abode
> Our souls arrive in peace."

The rest is a future rest.

But, in the *second* place, it is a PERFECT REST. It is complete in itself. In this world, no rest, however sweet, is perfect. When the Israelites entered the promised land, they found it was not all rest there. And we, who are under the Gospel, find it pretty much the same. There are cares that worry us, and thoughts that perplex us, and much to disturb us, in our most tranquil moments. But, in the heavenly Canaan, in the land above, that flows with milk and honey, there is complete rest; holiness and joy and pleasure are there for ever in perfection.

The rest there is perfect, *because it is free from sin.* Sin, which has such a terrible hold upon us here, shall have no power there. What a blessing this will be! Then we shall be freed from temptation! Now, the assaults of Satan try us very severely. We are often cast down. Many a time, like Peter of old, we are tempted to deny our Lord. Like Paul, we have our "thorn in the flesh." A sinful nature, a lying devil, an ensnaring world, are pronounced enemies of our souls. "When we would do good, evil is present with us." There is "another law in our members, warring against the law of our minds, and bringing us into captivity to the law of sin which is in our members." But, in God's perfect rest, all this shall have an end. We shall have no more to lead us astray; no more sin to ensnare us. We shall be free from sin, and so shall be able to enjoy perfect rest.

Sorrows, too, shall have an end. There shall be no grief or pain or death there. "God shall wipe away all tears from our eyes;" "we shall not sorrow any more at all." We shall sit down beside the still waters of Paradise, free from all tribulation, for the former things shall have passed away for ever, all things shall have become new.

And, thus, the rest of heaven shall be a *rest unmingled with evil*. Nought shall ever enter that blessed land to disturb the peace of God's people. There shall be no alloy of sin or suffering to mar our joy or happiness. There is freedom, life, gladness, light and glory. No evil shall distress the saints of the Lord; but, with hearts that know no grief, with souls that know no sin, they shall for ever rejoice in the perfect rest of that eternal home. They shall sing that new song—the song, the blessed words and music of which can only be learned in heaven.

And not only will the rest be perfect, because freed from all sin, all sorrow, and all evil, but, also, *because we shall be prepared to enjoy it*. The discipline that the soul undergoes in this world is to prepare it for the world to come. Not a command is given, or a trial sent, that has not this end in view. The materials are all prepared for the Temple before they are sent there. The corn is threshed and winnowed before it is stored away in the granary. And we are made ready before we are called away. We could not enjoy that rest if we were not thus prepared for it. In this life, we have no great joy, unless some sorrow goes before it. We should not enjoy the fresh and glorious beauties of the spring had we not passed through the rough and hard winter. We do not know the value of peace until we have contrasted it with the horrors of war. Nor do we properly appreciate health till we know what sickness is. And, when we reach yon happy land, we could not value its blessed rest unless we could look back upon a life spent here in the wilderness, in gloom, and war, and pain. It is the pruning that helps the vine. It is blow upon blow that forms the rough marble into shape. It is the bitter medicine that makes the sick man well. And all this preparation we shall have gone through before we enter the rest that remaineth to the people of God.

And as the soul is prepared, so will the body be. These weak, corruptible, mortal bodies shall be changed, and endued with power, and glory, and honour, and immortality. Now, they are bodies adapted to this world—this animal life; then, they will be bodies adapted to the other world—the spiritual life. Whatever may be the joys or the duties of heaven, we shall have souls and bodies specially prepared for those joys and duties. What those bodies will be like we know not: "It doth not yet appear what we shall be; but we know that when He shall appear we shall be like Him; for we shall see Him as He is." And thus the rest will be more perfect because we shall be prepared for it.

But, above all things else, the perfection of that rest will consist in the glorious fact that there we shall ever be with the Lord. Within the celestial city dwells the Saviour and Redeemer of mankind, and there we shall dwell with Him. There shall be safely gathered in all those who here below have loved the Lord Jesus in sincerity and in truth. There they shall be in the immediate presence of God; yielding adoration to Him that sitteth on the throne, to the Lamb that here was led to the slaughter, but that now reigneth; with whom we shall reign, after we have run this comfortless race through this miserable earthly vale. We cannot yet look back on the journey finished, the warfare accomplished, the race run to the end, the prize won. We know not what it is to behold our Master and Redeemer face to face. Yet, have we not in the Gospel rest some foretastes of what it will be when we shall rest in His presence, in the home of His glory? Do we not with the eye of faith behold Him who is the altogether lovely, the chiefest among ten thousand? But what is this compared with the future, when we shall see Him as He is? Now, we know that "eye hath not seen, nor ear heard, neither hath entered into the heart of man the things which God hath prepared for them that love Him." Hereafter, the eye of sight shall behold His face in righteousness, shall behold His kingdom and His glory. Nothing shall interrupt our communion with Him. " There shall be no night there " —the " perpetual presence of Christ with His saints makes it always one noon of light and glory." We shall drink of the rivers of His pleasure that are at His right hand. We shall refresh ourselves in the full springs of life, light and joy, and rest in the perfect rest of the new Jerusalem—the glorious city of our God.

What more can be needed to complete that rest? No sin, no sorrow, no evil in it; souls and bodies prepared especially to enjoy it; the full presence of Christ in the midst of His people—is not this all that we can wish for? Could we desire more? Is not the rest which remaineth for the people of God a perfect rest?

In the *third* place, that rest is an ETERNAL REST.

It is forever and forever. It shall never have an end. Rest in this world is not for long. Though the night succeed the day of toil, the night in its turn is followed by the day. There is no lasting rest. But, beyond the grave, we shall enter into an eternal rest. We shall never leave that blessed home. We shall never tread the wilderness path again. Storm and tempest shall all be over. Tribulation and sorrow, temptation and sin, oppression and persecution, shall cease. There shall be no more doubts and fears, no more deep questionings and heart burnings, no more weary toil and unsatisfied desires. All this shall have passed away—lost in the river of death—and we shall never meet them again. We shall enter into rest.

The Word of God secures this blessed hope to us again and again. God will give, says St. Paul, "to them who, by patient continuance in well-doing, seek for glory, and honour, and immortality, eternal life." "He that overcometh shall go no more out." "There shall be no more death, neither sorrow, nor crying, neither shall there be any more pain: for the former things have passed away." "We shall ever be with the Lord." Heaven would lose much of its happiness were it to have an end. But it is everlasting life. It is the fulness of joy for evermore.

> "For ever with the Lord:
> Amen, so let it be.
> Life from the dead is in that word,
> 'Tis immortality."

This must be a feature of that rest, full of comfort and hope, to the earnest, true Christian. Even should it lack that perfectness, of which I have been speaking, it will have enough of joy in it to render its perpetual endurance desirable. Every day, nay, every hour, will bring with it some new delight, some fuller development of heavenly pleasure. As the years roll by—years in which we shall never grow old—we shall become more and more capable of enjoying that rest; we shall see more glory, more power, more wisdom in the God and Lord of our souls; we shall go on and on, farther and still farther, into the ocean of His eternal and boundless love. All will be rest. Not mere idle rest, but an eternal cessation from the woes of this world, an eternal participation in the joys of heaven. There will be no change of state, no end, no termination to our blessedness. It will be an eternal rest.

Future, perfect, eternal—such are the characteristics of that rest which yet remaineth, into which, God grant, we may all enter! What a precious promise! What a glorious hope! But notice, this rest remaineth for *the people of God.* It is not for everybody. It is not for those who know not God. They have no part or lot in the matter. They have not carried the Cross, and they cannot expect to wear the Crown. Only those who have believed on the Lord Jesus shall enter into His rest. We may lose it through unbelief. The Israelites that perished in the wilderness could not enter into the promised rest of Canaan, because of unbelief. It may be the same with us in regard to the rest that still remains for God's people. "Let us labour, therefore, to enter into that rest, lest any man fall after the same example of unbelief." We must believe, we must obey, we must be steadfast, or we cannot enter heaven. We have no right to think we shall. We have no right to look forward to a place in that home of glory. "Except a man be born again, he cannot see the kingdom of God." "Not every one that saith unto me, Lord, Lord, shall enter into the kingdom of heaven; but he that doeth the will of my Father, which is in heaven." And, "this is the work of God, that ye believe on Him whom He hath sent." There is no other way into glory but this. There is no other title to heaven than this.

But, to those who are truly and indeed God's people, how sure is this promised rest. The God that cannot lie hath spoken it. We have the earnest of it now. In our deep sorrow, in the wearing sickness, in the moments of repentance and of communion with our Lord, we seem to be very near that rest. We almost see its glories, and hear the song of them that are already there. The cloud seems to break, and its dark, jutting points are touched with the roseate tints of the light of the better land. Many and many a bright ray struggles through the mist and cheers our sad, sorrowing, toiling lives. Yes, we get rich foretastes of heaven and of its rest even in this world. But, ere long, we shall behold and enjoy the reality. Our pilgrimage will soon be ended. We shall soon go into the dark night that shall hide this world from our sight. We shall soon stand on the brink of death's cold, gloomy river. Its heavy clouds shall chill our very soul. An unseen hand shall touch this weak, trembling flesh. It shall fall broken and destroyed. But, from its ruins, the spirit shall rise in all the fulness of its liberty. Away from those cold, cold waters shall it

THE LAST REST.

rise. The mists shall be passed. The cloud barriers shall be left behind. The morning of eternal glory shall dawn.

> "The morning shall awaken, the shadows shall decay,
> And each true-hearted servant shall shine as doth the day:
> There God, our King and Portion, in fulness of His grace,
> Shall we behold for ever, and worship face to face."

Oh that will be a glorious day to us when we shall realize all this! It will make amends for all we suffer here. We may now be often cast down, often perplexed, often in dismay. We may never have rest in this life. Do not seek it here! Our rest is future; it is beyond this heaving, restless world. Our rest is perfect; it has everything heart could wish for. Our rest is eternal; it shall never, never end. But it is in heaven. We have it not, and cannot have it in this life. "There remaineth, therefore, a rest to the people of God." May we learn this in all its fulness! May we, by God's grace, enter into the rest! May it be ours hereafter to have heaven for our home!

> "O sweet and blessed country, the home of God's elect!
> O sweet and blessed country, that eager hearts expect!
> Jesus, in mercy bring us to that dear land of rest:
> Who art, with God the Father and Spirit, ever bless'd."

SERMON XVI.

ASSURANCE.

ROMANS v. 8, 9.—" But God commendeth His love towards us, in that, while we were yet sinners, Christ died for us. Much more then, being now justified by His blood, we shall be saved from wrath through Him."

THE certainty of salvation is a source of great comfort to God's people. The assurance that not one jot or tittle of the many declarations contained in Scripture as to their redemption can possibly fail is a solid foundation on which the soul may rest—a living hope that may enkindle faith and engender devotion. If God has given the Christian a sense of this assurance—a firm persuasion that nought can ever separate him from his Father's love,—no matter how great the temptation may be, how severe the affliction, how rough and long the road of life, the darkest cloud will be tinged with glory, the gloomiest night will be radiant with hope. But we are so given to doubt, so prone to question, that oftentimes we have no certainty at all that we will ever attain to the bliss, which, at other times, we have hoped and striven for. We look into our hearts and we see so many hidden sins yet lurking in deep places; we examine our lives and we are so struck with the sad want of entire self-consecration, and before us arises such a consciousness of the lack of that simple faith, that childlike obedience so essential for the Christian to have, that we instinctively feel, that, with so many imperfections, so many sins, we are yet very very far from the kingdom of God, and without a hope or prospect of ever entering into the presence of the Lord of Hosts. This is the experience of very many Christians. They think so much of their shortcomings that they lose hope, and live uncertain as to what the future may be. Such a state of doubt is very detrimental to Christian growth and development. One of the great causes of it is from looking too much at self, and from the mistaken notion that our attainments enter into the question of our salvation. We are thinking of self and not of God. He, and His promises are forgotten. We dream of what we can do, and forget what He has done. This is wrong. No one can have an assurance of redemption so long as he looks only to himself. His good works form no sure ground of hope. They are simply as the sinking sand. The only hope, the only assurance, the only certainty of eternal life which he can have, must rest on God, and on God alone. He is the Rock of Ages on which we may safely build, and nothing—not even the conclaves of hell—shall ever prevail against that blessed company of faithful people whose present and future are in His hands, who are supported and upheld by His gracious and eternal purposes.

The Apostle, in my text, directs us to this ground of assurance. He rests everything on God—nothing on man. The atonement wrought by Christ is, he maintains, a strong bond of union between God and His people that nought can sever. He shows, that, by His sacrifice, our salvation is sure. He proves His proposition by reminding us, that when we were yet in sin, God gave His Son for us. "God commendeth His love towards us, in that while we were yet sinners, Christ died for us. Much more then, being now justified by His blood, we shall be saved from wrath, through Him." The argument is reiterated and expanded in the next verse : " For if, when we were enemies, we were reconciled to God by the death of His Son, much more being reconciled, we shall be saved by His life." The ground of our assurance is then based on the sacrifice of Christ. And we can see how sure this ground is by calling to mind the nature of the sacrifice. Let us, therefore, in the *first* place look at THE COSTLINESS OF CHRIST'S SACRIFICE.

It was a sacrifice more than equivalent to the worth of the whole human family. The vast universe of God had nothing greater to give. There was no being but One in heaven or earth who was qualified to fulfil the requirements of the law and to die for man. Nothing but the sacrifice of Christ was able to redeem our fallen race from the penalty we had incurred. And such a sacrifice *cost much love.* Nothing but love could have induced God to give up His only begotten Son—the brightness of His glory, and the express image of His person—as a ransom for the sins of His people. They had rebelled against Him. They had forfeited every claim to His consideration. They deserved nought less than repudiation and banishment from His presence and favour for ever. But the sin which had called into action the justice did not impair the love. He loved His poor, weak fallen children in spite of what they had done. He showed His love by giving over unto death the sinless and innocent Jesus. "In this was manifested the love of God toward us, because that God sent His only begotten Son into the world that we might live through Him." It cost Him much love to do this—to give up one so near and dear to Him, partaking of His very nature, for the redemption of rebels deserving only of eternal death. Not a spark of love in our cold, dead souls towards Him, and yet He provides for us a full and free salvation. "Herein is love, not that we loved God, but that He loved us and sent His Son to be the propitiation for our sins." Surely, if in our sins we still retained the love of God; if in our fallen state God sacrificed His Son for us—a sacrifice costing so much love can never go for nought.

But besides love the sacrifice *cost much suffering.* Who can tell the sufferings of Christ? Truly He was "a man of sorrows and acquainted with grief;"

wounded and bruised in the mill of affliction. The humiliation consequent upon His laying aside His majesty, and taking upon Himself our nature, with its infirmities and destinies, of itself cost much suffering. Look at the life here on earth. When, after thirty years of obscurity, in Joseph's house, the glory of God was manifested in Him at the time of His baptism, it was but, as it were, the light that should lead Him into a ministry of sad disappointment and of trying deprivation. Three years homeless, without a place to lay His head, He wandered from city to city throughout the length and breadth of the land, preaching the Gospel of peace and salvation amid the sneers and persecution of the Jews, the suspicions of His friends, and the doubts of His disciples. And when at the last His hour was come, when the great work of His life should be accomplished, how great the grief then! Who dare lift up the veil of night that covers the sufferings in Gethsemane? Who could disperse the gloom that shrouded the land in darkness as the blood of the sacrifice was being offered up from the cross? Great, indeed, and costly must have been a sacrifice that entailed so much suffering. Those nail-pierced hands, that thorn-circled brow, that spear-rivened side, were not endured by the weak and sensitive God-man without much pain. The agony and bloody sweat endured in the garden, the death-cry at the last, were but the outward signs of a deep inward struggle. Laden with the sins of the whole world, dying the cruelest of all deaths, no tongue can describe—no heart can conceive—the intense suffering of the Lamb of God. We shall never understand it. Eternity cannot tell the story. If the sacrifice of Christ cost so much suffering, can we suppose for a moment that its object will not be gained?

But besides the cost of love and the cost of suffering, the sacrifice of Christ *cost much preparation*. The fall of man was such that an immediate recovery was impossible. It was necessary that man should be made to realize what a terrible thing sin is and more especially unatoned sin. The penalty of the broken law, consisting of utter estrangement from God, must be seen by man before God can remove that penalty by substitution. Therefore from the fall to the advent a long time elapsed. The world was gradually prepared for the era of its redemption. Nations were born and died, empires appeared and vanished, the affairs of the wide world were under the direct guidance of God, and everything was made to tend Christward. A nation was chosen to preserve on the earth the knowledge of the true God. To them were committed the types and promises of the atonement. By stupendous miracles they were cared for and preserved amid the changes of long centuries. Priests and prophets were raised up to impress upon the people the truth of the coming Messiah. The sacrifices preserved the grand fact that without the shedding of blood there could be no remission of sin. And while no doubt the world was being prepared so was the Lamb under preparation for the sacrifice. The whole plan of redemption, its conditions and terms, were prepared in the Divine mind. The earthly life of the Messiah, ordered from all eternity, was but a further preparation for the salvation of the world. Shall all this preparation fail? Shall the work of God as shown in preparing the way for the Christ be of none effect? Shall His power be after all but impotent weakness? Surely this cost of preparation must tend to enhance the value of the sacrifice.

And when we remember the costliness of the sacrifice as shown in the love, the suffering and the preparation it called for, have we not a very firm foundation on which to rest the assurance of our salvation? Can the price paid for our redemption fail to satisfy the demands of the law? Is all the costliness of the atonement thrown away? Oh no! In the very costliness of the sacrifice we can be assured of the future. We can rest in it. We can hope in it. We can rejoice in it. God's greatest gift to man cannot be thrown away. The love will not be lost, the suffering will not be in vain, the preparation will not be useless. The sacrifice will not be brought to nought!

But in the *second* place, in considering the nature of Christ's sacrifice, let us look at the EXTENT OF THE SACRIFICE.

For whom did Christ die ? St. Paul tells us that Christ died for the ungodly. Christ Himself says, " I came not to call the righteous but sinners to repentance." We gather from the character of those who are invited for whom Christ died. " Ho, every one that thirsteth, come ye to the waters, and he that hath no money, come ye, buy and eat ; yea come buy wine and milk without money and without price." Here it is the poor and needy who are called upon to partake of the blessings of the Gospel. Of such Christ said, " Blessed are they which do hunger and thirst after righteousness: for they shall be filled." Again He calls unto Him the weary and the heavy laden, promising to them rest unto their souls. So He proclaims " If any man thirst, let him come unto me and drink." And among the last messages of the Holy Ghost to the Church, the gracious invitation is given, " Let him that is athirst come ; and whosoever will, let him take the water of life freely." We see then that it is the ungodly, those who are sinners, the poor and needy, the hungry and thirsty, the weary and the heavy laden —yea whosoever will—that are invited to avail themselves of the redemption wrought by Christ. It was for these Christ died, it was to these the benefits of the sacrifice were extended. It was only these who needed salvation ; it was only for those who needed it that a ransom was offered.

Now if we would have an assurance of salvation, we need but ask, are we among the sort of people invited ? Do we feel that we are sinners ; are we weary with the heavy burden of sin ; do we hunger and thirst after righteousness ? Then are the benefits of the sacrifice ours. If we have not this sense of sin and want, then have we no part or lot in the matter. No one can be saved who does not realize the want of salvation. But those who have this want are called of God; for them Christ died.

And yet what of those who feel their need of a Saviour—who have reached that state in which they are simply helpless, and without hope of ever reaching heaven ? Everything seems to bar up the way to God ; there is no light, no bright future. An offended God and well-merited punishment is all that stands before them. They long with an irrepressible longing for reconciliation with their Father. As returning prodigals they would be glad of but one small glance of love that might cheer their deep sad hearts. But it is "guilty, guilty, guilty," that rings in their ears. It is a broken law that gives strength to the sharp sting of conscience with which the soul is wounded. It is a sense of estrangement from God that makes the soul aware of the awful gloom of the dark night of sin. How dare they look up to God? How dare they think of heaven? But oh, it is just such as these that Jesus calls to Him. It is these that He invites to drink of the waters of salvation. It was for these that He poured out His life-blood as an atoning sacrifice before the mercy-seat of God. He died for sinners and for none but sinners. He redeemed them from eternal wrath; He made up for them a spotless robe of righteousness in which they might stand without sin in the great and terrible day of the Lord. Oh, what an assurance of salvation there is in all this for poor, way-worn, needy sinners! The sacrifice for us—for all who feel that they are sinners! Just the very thing we want—salvation full and free for everybody through the blood of the Lamb! What a grand foundation on which to rest the future!

And behold just here another ground of assurance. The gospel invitation is a very broad one. Salvation is offered to all mankind freely and right royally. It is "whosoever will" that may come. Do we want to be saved? Then most certainly we will be saved. The very want of our souls, the will to come to Christ, is an assurance of salvation. For we do not will these things of ourselves. "It is God which worketh in you both to will and to do of His good pleasure." So then the will is planted by God. He has begun the good work. And in this we may be assured of the future; "being confident," as the Apostle says, " of this very thing, that He which hath begun a good work in you will perform, or finish, it until the day of Jesus Christ." And depend upon it God would never give the will, if the want could not be satisfied. He would never call upon us to partake of a salvation which did not actually belong to us. It is because it is ours that we are called to it. It is because the blood of Christ was poured out for us, that we have the will to wash in the cleansing fountain. And if for us, then may we rest confidently in the assurance of Christ "Those that Thou gavest me I have kept, and none of them is lost;" "no one is able to pluck them out of My hands." We are safe in Christ, and if so " there is no condemnation for them that are in Christ Jesus."

In all this there is abundant cause for a sense of security. The sacrifice extends to us. If God be true, then is our salvation absolutely sure. We are included in the terms of the atonement, and if we accept those terms there is no possibility of our being lost. Heaven and earth may pass away, but God's word cannot pass away. The blood of the sacrifice was offered up for every one of God's people, and if then we are justified by His blood we shall be saved from wrath through Him. Trembling, doubting one, here is hope, nay positive assurance! Your Father bids you come and be at rest. Your Saviour has removed from you the condemnation of the law, by dying for you. Oh, rest upon this grand truth! Your life may be gladdened by it; your death may be brightened by it! Turn from self and look to Christ. Build your future upon His sacrifice. It cannot fail you for it was for you He died. Here is a sure ground of hope, an assurance that this painful life ended you will rise to the life immortal through Him who loved you and gave Himself for you. If we feel our need of a Saviour, then may we be sure beyond a doubt that He is ours. At this glorious assurance we can bid the clouds of doubt disperse, and can command the sea of Satanic opposition to divide that we may pass through on our journey to the Promised Land of Eternal Rest without let or hindrance.

In the *third and last place* let us look at the EFFICACY OF THE SACRIFICE.

What did the Sacrifice accomplish? How far did it go to save man? This is a most important question. Nor can there be a full assurance unless this point be satisfactorily settled. If we cannot be sure that the sacrifice of Christ wrought a full and complete salvation, so that there remains nothing for us to do more than to accept it, we shall forever be in doubt as to what we have to do and how far we have done it. There are some people who hold that the salvation is but partial—that much remains for man to do. Christ they say did not altogether save man from the wrath to come. They will not allow that His sacrifice needs nothing more to perfect it. And yet there is nothing plainer than this fact that if the sacrifice of Christ is not perfect in itself we have no power whatever of adding to it. When God charged our first parents not to eat of the tree of knowledge He declared that in the day they did eat thereof they should surely die. And the sentence did not fail of fulfilment. The poison of sin killed the soul. It was henceforth dead, and if dead it was incapable of action. Now the death of Christ was for the very purpose of giving life to man. " For as in Adam all die, even so in Christ shall all be made alive." It would not have been the least possible use for Christ to have died unless He had altogether brought back these dead souls of ours to life. It would be no use to tie a rope around a drowning man and then leave him to get out of the water himself. A dead stump though planted in a rich fertile soil, exposed to the genial rays of the sun and tended by the most skilful of gardeners, would never bud and flower and produce fruit. It needs these things but it also needs life. And so does man, and unless the death of Christ brought him life, it stands to reason that he can never get it of himself. And what do the best of our good works amount to ? Have we ever done anything to atone for the sins of the past ? Are we fit to enter into the presence of God ? No, no, man cannot save himself. It was God's purpose in sending Christ into the world to save man. And when He saves He saves altogether. It is not for sinful man to stand beside the Almighty in this work. There is no need of it. It was a full, perfect and sufficient sacrifice. It wants nothing to finish it. The work is all done—done long, long ago. The efficacy of the sacrifice was absolute and able to wash away all sin. There remains nothing for man to do. The declaration of a dying Saviour proclaimed to a ransomed world that the whole work of salvation was finished. The sting of sin lost its power in the wound it inflicted in our Blessed Redeemer. All our sins were borne in His body on the accursed tree. And if He has borne them, why should we bear them? If He has paid the penalty are not we then free? How plainly the Scriptures speak on this point! "The blood of Jesus Christ cleanseth from all sin." "Though your sins be as scarlet, they shall be as white as snow; though they be red like crimson, they shall be as wool." "We have redemption through the blood of Christ, the forgiveness of sins according to the riches of His grace." And when we remember these grand and glorious statements all bearing on the question of the efficacy of the sacrifice we cannot but assent to the deduction of St. Paul: "Therefore, we conclude that a man is justified by faith without the deeds of the law;" "for by the works of the law shall no flesh be justified."

Now this is a grand ground of assurance. There could be no better. We need only to embrace the offer, and we are sure of salvation. It does not rest upon us but upon Christ. Everything is in and with Christ. As the Apostle says, "I am crucified with Christ; nevertheless I live; yet not I, but Christ liveth in me: and the life which I now live in the flesh I live by the faith of the Son of God, who loved me and gave Himself for me." What a firm foundation on which to rest!

> "Mine is the sin, but thine the righteousness;
> Mine is the guilt, but thine the cleansing blood:
> Here is my robe, my refuge, and my peace—
> Thy blood, Thy righteousness, O Lord, my God."

That blood will wash every one to whom it is applied, so that nought of sin will remain. That robe of righteousness will cover all, and in Christ Jesus we shall stand spotless before the throne of God. Depend upon it, the efficacy of the sacrifice goes to the very root of the matter. The work was done once and for all thoroughly and absolutely. Nor will any part of it be lost. God would not attempt that which He could not accomplish; nor is there anything beyond His power. All things are possible with Him, and there can be no doubt whatever of the thorough efficacy of the sacrifice by which He reconciled His people unto Himself, and fulfilled the minutest and the greatest requirements of the law.

We may, then, confidently assert, in view of the nature of the sacrifice, that we have a positive ground of assurance. This sacrifice was offered up for our salvation. We see how, from its costliness, its extent and its efficacy, it cannot fall short of what it was intended to accomplish. All that love, and suffering, and preparation, will not be lost. We can depend upon that. Nor need we have any fear as to our individual salvation. If we feel our need of it we may be very sure we are included in it. If we want Christ it is because He wants us. And this is not all. God wants us just as we are to come unto Him—without preparation, nothing doubting but that the whole work is done—done once and for all, done most efficiently, most thoroughly. Original sin, actual sin, sins past and sins to come, are atoned for by the sacrifice of Christ. He who could save the dying thief simply upon his repentance and faith can save us. We may be assured of all this.

There is no reason whatever for doubts on our part! We may be positively sure of salvation. We may be absolutely certain that hereafter we will enter heaven. But the assurance must be placed, not in ourselves, but in God. All our hopes must rest on Christ. He must be All and in all; the Alpha and Omega, the First and the Last! It must be the free and boundless mercy, the unfathomable love of an eternal and infinite Father! That is the only Rock on which we can build the future; the only ground in which the anchor of hope may find a firm hold! And who can doubt that love? Who can question it? For "God commendeth His love toward us, in that while we were yet sinners, Christ died for us. Much more then, being now justified by His blood, we shall be saved from wrath through Him." There is the love binding us to God, a bond infinitely increased by the sacrifice of Christ. With that love, that sacrifice no child of God can ever be lost. We may say with the sainted Wesley:

> "O, love, thou bottomless abyss!
>   My sins are swallowed up in thee;
> Covered is my unrighteousness,
>   Nor spot of guilt remains on me;
> While Jesus' blood through earth and skies,
> Mercy, free boundless mercy, cries."

CHRISTIAN READER,

It may be God has made these poor and feeble words of mine a blessing to your soul. Remember, then, your duty. Let the good news that has made you glad be given by you to some poor perishing one, that he, too, may share the blessing. Speak a word to those around you of the dear Saviour that is able to save them from eternal misery! Oh, work for Jesus! Say something for Him wherever you are! It is a blessed thing to do. It is a blessed thing to lead a sinner to the Lord. The world is full of those who know not the way of salvation. In a few short years—who knows but ere many days?—both you and I will be called away to our rest, and we shall have to leave this glorious work, and never, never again speak a word that shall save a soul from death! What a solemn thought! Then let us speak now! If this book has been in any sense a blessing to you, do your part to make it a blessing to others.

www.ingramcontent.com/pod-product-compliance
Lightning Source LLC
Chambersburg PA
CBHW021012240426
43669CB00037B/598